Trails to Testimony

Praise for *Trails to Testimony*

I strongly believe that all the YM leaders in the stake and bishoprics and all Scouting parents should read this book. Brother Harris shares such a clear message of what it is really all about and I cannot recommend this book more highly. The charts, comparisons, stories, quotes, and scripture references in this book are invaluable!

K. Hansen–Kansas

I recently bought and read Mr. Harris' book "Trails to Testimony". . . what an *excellent* piece of work!! I am a new Scoutmaster in a Ward with a very weak scouting program and this book has inspired and strengthened me to do what I know will be difficult in our program - influence change.

J. Jones–Utah

Stakes can feel completely comfortable using the principles taught in Brad's book as a text for Little Philmonts, as a training outline for bishopric training or of YM leaders. I'm seeing whole stakes buying several books at a time and distributing them at stake training meetings and council commissioner colleges to LDS scouters as well as non-members who work with LDS units. It is the definitive resource on LDS Scouting and a wonderful tool for parents. Readers will experience 'A-ha moments' throughout and will develop a deeper appreciation and understanding of how LDS scouting can be the vehicle of bringing young men to Christ.

J. Woodwell–Texas

I bought this book between weekends of Wood Badge. This book took everything that they taught me and put it into the LDS program. Every Scout's parent would benefit from this book!!! It explains each part of the program along with goals, aims and methods of each program in Scouting (Cubs, Scouts, Varsity and Venturing). It spells out each of the programs principles easily. I wish that this book had been handed to me with my calling because I would have spent a ton less time beating my head against the wall trying to stress over the little things. I recommend this book to everyone whether in the Scouting program for a long time or a short time. Bishops and Stake Presidents would benefit from reading this book too.

C. Fisher–Texas

As a mother of a recently turned 12 year old boy, I loved reading this book! It explains how Scouting is supposed to help my boys become great men. I hope that all Young Men leaders and Scouting leaders will take the time to read this book and learn how they can help the boys in their charge, no matter the size of their quorums. Scouting can bring boys to Christ if a few basic principles are followed which this book outlines excellently.

J. Fincher–Utah

Trails to Testimony

Bringing Young Men to Christ
Through Scouting

Bradley D. Harris

Acknowledgments

I'd like to thank the many who have given me insight and help as I have written this book—among them Clint Lawton, Doug Livingston, Joseph Woodwell, Jack Haycock, Mark Allen, Bill Bouska, Michael Law, Tom Smallwood, Michael Marchese, Jerry Dees, Ralph Wappel, Jennifer Brown, John Kapololu, Paula Sherrill, Ryan Howells, Erik Rytting, Patti Freeman, Dave Carlson, Todd Moody, Star Hall, and Robert Workman. Special thanks go to my students in BYU's Scouting in the Church class.

Thane Packer was one of my professors at BYU in the late 1970s. Several years later when his book, *On My Honor,* was published, I read it and I was amazed at how he could draw on so many experiences to illustrate his points and to describe his perspective on Scouting in the Church.

From 1998 to 2003, while working for the National Council of the Boy Scouts of America, I was invited by local councils to train volunteers and professionals. I met with LDS leaders around the country, heard their questions, felt their frustrations, and listened to their stories of success. From 2006 to 2009, I served on the Young Mens General Board of the LDS Church. While on the board I visited over 100 Aaronic Priesthood quorums and dozens of stakes and wards around the country. Recently, it dawned on me that I now had the experience and perspective that Thane Packer had twenty years earlier. Just as he inspired thousands to more fully implement Scouting as the activity arm of the Aaronic Priesthood, I hope to update and inspire a new generation of adult leaders in the Church.

My eternal thanks go to Dad, Mom, and my three brothers. Additionally, this book would not be possible without my wife, Sandy. She spent many hours with me encouraging, listening, giving perspective, and editing. Her encouragement and belief in me lifts me always.

Contents

"There is no more significant work in this world than the preparation of boys to become men of capacity, of strength, of integrity, who are qualified to live productive and meaningful lives."

(Gordon B. Hinckley, "Fireside Marks Boy Scouts of America 75th Birthday," Ensign, April 1985, 76.)

Introduction

Several years ago while serving on the national staff of the Boy Scouts of America, I was asked by the Association of Baptists for Scouting to speak about Venturing at their annual convention in Asheville, North Carolina—a beautiful retreat setting surrounded by pine trees, azaleas, and rhododendrons. I entered the main hall thirty minutes before my presentation was scheduled to begin so I could watch the proceedings. Speaker after speaker spoke passionately about Scouting; some pounded the pulpit or raised their voices to illustrate a point. This usually prompted a "Hallelujah!" from several in the audience. I decided that I would attempt to evoke a similar response when it was my turn to speak.

After a brief introduction, I stepped up to the podium and began to quote Matthew 6:33, "But seek ye first the kingdom of God, and His righteousness; and [I raised my voice] all these things shall be added unto you." I lightly pounded the pulpit for emphasis. "Hallelujah!" came several responses from the back of the room. The energy in the room was palpable as the listeners heard something that inspired them.

Although it is not an LDS custom to exclaim "Hallelujah!" in our meetings, we do experience "hallelujah" moments. This book is a collection of observations and quiet "hallelujahs" I have experienced during three decades of working with Aaronic Priesthood leaders, parents, and youth.

In my first five years at Brigham Young University, I taught three courses in Scouting education. As I developed the curriculum for a class called "Scouting in the Church," I realized that Aaronic Priesthood leaders and parents could benefit from the information contained in the course. This book, then, summarizes the research and information I collected for that course. Through this book, I hope to help parents and the nearly 80,000 Aaronic Priesthood/Scouting leaders in the United States use Scouting as a tool to help bring 400,000 Aaronic Priesthood young men to Christ by introducing them to the trails leading to testimony.

In my role as a Scouting professional for more than twenty years, I have seen the magic of the Scouting program when implemented properly—building character and leadership; challenging young people to greater achievement; and blessing the lives of youth, adults, and families. I have also seen many Scouting programs that held no magic; leaders and parents casually approached this inspired program as if it were just another assignment to be completed. It is this gap—this Grand Canyon of potential between the "magical" and the "mundane"—that has compelled me to collect my thoughts and observations.

From its beginning, Scouting has emphasized spirituality and religious values. Scouting founder Lord Robert Baden-Powell said, "There is no religious 'side' of the movement. The whole of it is based on religion, that is, on the realization and service of God. Let us, therefore, in training our Scouts, keep the higher aims in the forefront, not let ourselves get too absorbed in the steps. Don't let the technical outweigh the moral. . . . Our objective in the Scout movement is to give such help as we can in bringing about God's kingdom on earth."(www.scouting.org/media/relationships/scoutsabbathservices/badenpowell.aspx)

The hope of training the young men of the Church to "keep their higher aims in the forefront" convinced the First Presidency in 1911 to send a delegation led by Bryant Hinckley (President Gordon B. Hinckley's father) to Washington, D.C., to investigate Scouting. The flexibility and autonomy afforded by the Boy Scouts of America allowed the Church to implement the program to meet its needs, and the spiritual dimension promoted by Scouting was a perfect fit with the Aaronic Priesthood. As a result of this compatibility, in 1913 the Church formally adopted Scouting as the activity arm of the Aaronic Priesthood.

I believe that many Scouting programs have drifted from their original spiritual core over the years and have evolved into a group of boys and young men who are simply seeking awards. I hope that this book will aid parents and leaders in rediscovering the spiritual dimension of Scouting, and help them utilize Scouting to bring young men to Christ. In the back of the book you will find several pages on which you can write your spiritual impressions—your own "hallelujah moments."

Chapter 1: A Holy and Sacred Calling

As boys and young men strive to understand how to prepare for, worthily receive, and honor the Aaronic Priesthood, they need the help and guidance of caring and loving adults. Much of this help can and should come from parents and a home environment that fosters the truths of the gospel. Under the direction of priesthood leaders, instructors of priesthood quorums and Primary classes also teach, strengthen, and support the incorporation of gospel truths in the lives of boys and young men.

Priesthood and Primary leaders are not alone in their stewardship for boys and young men. Parents and adult leaders share this sacred responsibility.

THE ROLE OF PARENTS
According to *The Family: A Proclamation to the World*, it is parents who have the sacred duty of providing for and rearing their children in righteousness and of teaching those children to be law-abiding citizens who obey the commandments of God and who value service (see *Ensign*, Nov. 1995, 102). And as stated in the *Fulfilling My Duty To God: For Aaronic Priesthood Holders*, parents play a key role in helping their young men strengthen their testimony and their relationship with Heavenly Father, learn about and fulfill their priesthood duties, and apply the standards from *For the Strength of Youth*. (See *Fulfilling My Duty to God*, 2010, pg. 94). The materials and programs offered by the Church are designed to assist parents—not take the place of parents—as they help their children develop the skills and attributes needed to succeed in life

Following are some ways you as parents can help your sons receive the greatest benefit from the Church's youth programs:

- Become familiar with the *Fulfilling My Duty to God: For Aaronic Priesthood Holders* booklet; especially the section titled, To Quorum Advisers and Parents.

- The *Fulfilling My Duty to God* booklet reminds parents, "Focus on what the young men are becoming… the Duty to God book should not be seen as a list of tasks that the young men must hurry through in order to earn an award."

- Review *For the Strength of Youth* with your sons.

- Talk with your sons' Aaronic Priesthood and Scouting leaders. Learn what these leaders are doing on activity night and on campouts to help strengthen your son physically, mentally, and spiritually.

- Whenever you can, participate with your sons in Church youth events.

The Role of Adult Leaders

It is a holy and sacred calling to work with the young men in the Church. Young men need dedicated adult advisers who truly care about them. You will have the opportunity of helping young men at a critical time in their lives—a time when they are making crucial decisions that have eternal consequences. You have the opportunity to help create memories and establish a spiritual base that will be with them forever and that can put them on the trail to testimony.

Speaking to young men, Elder Jeffrey R. Holland described the effects that a good leader can have on a boy:

> I was your age once and you have never been mine. I remember what it was like and I did not fully appreciate what a legion of leaders, a host of leaders, a nation of leaders did for me as a Scout. . . .
>
> Here today, and tomorrow and last week and next month and forever, we pray there will be leaders who will invest themselves in the next generation and pass the torch of liberty and love and loyalty and service and devotion and reverence to you.
>
> I am the beneficiary of those kinds of leaders and so are you. The principles and virtues, the laws, the oaths, the mottos, the emblems, the symbols, the statement of scouting . . . is 45 years more important to me now than the day I received my eagle" (www.scoutmedia.org).

You may not receive feedback from the young men during your tenure as their leader, but at some point either in this life or the next, your name will be called blessed for the work you did and for the way it impacted those you served. A BYU student and Eagle Scout named Casey described to me the influence of his teacher's quorum adviser:

> My teacher's quorum adviser was fun and respectful. In fact, I always remember him teaching us to be respectful. I remember on my mission always thinking what he taught us about respecting people even when they were not the most respectful back to us. I learned some lifelong lessons, and he probably has no clue how much he affected me.

Having this kind of impact on young men doesn't happen by accident. We need to prepare ourselves. The scriptures admonish us to learn our duty (see D&C 107:99). Duty requires that we learn and then apply what we have learned. However, is duty enough of a motivation to ensure success with young men? Do the young men feel that you care only because you were called to care? Or do they believe you care for them regardless of your current calling?

Love is a stronger, deeper motivation than duty. To work effectively with young men, we must serve out of love. Young men know if they are truly loved. They know whether their adviser really cares for them or is just fulfilling his duty.

Think back on your Aaronic Priesthood/Scouting experience as a young man. Which of your leaders come to mind? Why? If you created a hall of honor in your home containing the pictures of the men and women who made the greatest impact on your life, who would be on that wall? Almost certainly, they would be the leaders who truly cared about you.

THE ROLE OF THE BISHOPRIC

Church leaders also need to ensure that they call effective leaders. The call to serve in the Aaronic Priesthood with young men requires valiant effort and enthusiasm. Previous experience with young men is important, but not critical, because previous experience does not guarantee success. (In fact, it can actually hinder, as will be discussed in Chapter 11.) When considering calling a man with previous experience, you as a bishop should contact previous priesthood leaders and ask open-ended questions to determine if the man was a worthy and successful leader. Success should not be measured completely by the number of Eagle Scouts or merit badges earned by the young men. True success in leading young men can be determined by asking:

- What were indications that the young men trusted him?

- Did they look up to him as a spiritual leader?

- What are some examples that show that the young men were willing to confide in him?

- Describe how activity nights went—were they well-attended? Did he apply priesthood lessons in weekday activities?

- Did the leader train young men how to lead and then allow them to lead, or did he do most of the work himself?

As the presidency of the Aaronic Priesthood in the ward, the bishopric plays a key role in the overall success of the Aaronic Priesthood and Scouting programs. Working closely together and under the direction of the Spirit, the bishopric has the power, influence, and mantle to call the best men to serve with the young men.

According to President Thomas S. Monson, the influence of an Aaronic Priesthood advisor is far-reaching and immeasurable. For this reason, he encourages local priesthood leaders to seek men for that calling who are worthy of emulation (see "Seven Steps to Success with Aaronic Priesthood Youth," *Ensign*, Feb. 1985, 22).

Bishop C. Frederick Pingel of the Beavercreek Ward, Dayton Ohio East Stake, spoke in the October 1982 priesthood session of general conference and described the importance of calling effective leaders. He told bishops that as they organize a new ward, they should first "identify your best man and make him your Scoutmaster. . . . Brethren, don't sacrifice here. I don't know where to tell you to sacrifice, but don't do it here. Put truly fine people in your youth programs ("Activating Young Men of the Aaronic Priesthood," *Ensign*, Nov. 1982, 35).

In 1983 a new ward was created in Philomath, Oregon. The new bishop prayerfully chose two counselors, an executive secretary, and a ward clerk (that was me). With our new ward list in hand, the new bishopric met with the task of prayerfully filling all other positions in the ward. At that point, no one on the list of more than sixty active families had a calling in the new ward. The wise bishop announced that of the more than 100 positions needing to be filled, the first position to be filled would be the Scoutmaster and deacons quorum adviser. Wouldn't it be great if each new ward took advantage of an opportunity like this?

Sixteen years later while serving as a bishop in Texas, I applied this method. This time we had a fully functioning ward. I told my counselors to review the ward list and to not discount anyone because of their current calling. I stressed the idea that every worthy man in the ward was a prospect. After much prayer and discussion we agreed that Brother Christiansen would make the best Scoutmaster. He had three teenaged sons, had a great relationship with the young men in the ward, had served a successful mission, had a supportive wife, had steady employment, and was worthy. As a bonus, he loved the outdoors and was in excellent physical health. At the time he was serving on the stake high council. The stake president was very gracious and allowed him to be released. Not all Church callings work out this way, of course. The principle here is that we must look at every opportunity when it comes to finding the right person to serve with the young men.

Bishop H. David Burton, presiding bishop of the Church emphasizes the fact that although bishops need to delegate many of their responsibilities to appropriate leaders, there are some responsibilities they cannot delegate—and one of those is their direct responsibility for the young men of the Aaronic Priesthood. I learned as bishop that sometimes the needs and issues of the adults in the ward cried out louder for my attention than did those of the youth. Many times I was too quick to respond to the "urgent" cries for help from adults and too often delayed the "important" tasks related to the youth.

I am grateful to the bishoprics who served me as I was growing up; the many dedicated leaders they called are the ones who helped me discover the trail to testimony.

A Boy's Man

Looking back on my Aaronic Priesthood years, I believe that most of my adult advisers were truly interested in magnifying their calling on my behalf. I remember the men that took time away from their jobs and their families to go on weekend camping trips and to spend a week at summer camp with Troop 81. Each of these men had unique personality traits and spiritual qualities that I admired and tried to emulate.

One man who holds a prominent place in my hall of honor is Larry Reynolds, my priest quorum adviser. He truly loved each of the priests in the quorum. He was enthusiastic about the Church and his full-time mission experience. He went out of his way to spend time with us outside the required Church meetings on Sunday and our weeknight activities. He invited us over to his home on Sunday evenings. The combination of missionary stories, unconditional love, and ice cream played a major role in my decision to serve a mission. None of the fathers of the young men in the quorum had served missions. They encouraged us, but didn't have first-hand experience. But Brother Reynolds had that direct experience. The personality, the enthusiasm, and the spirit of Larry Reynolds contributed to that "mighty change of heart" we all needed to be dynamic missionaries. Brother Reynolds wrote to each of us on our missions. I knew by his words and actions that he loved me. He was a perfect example of the counsel in the scriptures: "And if any man among you be strong in the Spirit, let him take with him that is weak, that he may be edified in all meekness, that he may become strong also" (D&C 84:106).

Twenty-seven years later I found Brother Reynolds while on a business trip to Kansas City, where I spent a wonderful evening with him and his wife, Jolene. I discovered that Brother Reynolds was still young at heart—and was still working with young men. For more than a quarter of a century, the young men in the wards where he lived had been blessed as I was by this dedicated leader.

Brother Reynolds is what President Thomas S. Monson calls a "boy's man." As President Monson describes it, a "boy's man" loves the boys; he thinks like the boys; he is fun to be around. He maintains his place on the pedestal in the minds of the young men, and communicates to the boys by his actions and his words: "I like being with you." "You have great potential." "We can talk about anything, and I will not judge you." A "boy's man" also has a finely tuned spiritual antenna, ready at any time to find a spiritual application for a temporal activity.

Building boys is a noble and sacred effort. It requires the best efforts of dedicated men and women who have been called to serve. Building boys requires that we sanctify our lives in accordance with the gospel, consecrate our time and talents to saving souls, and magnify our callings. Building boys requires that we utilize every tool available.

The tools in an Aaronic Priesthood leader's toolbox include the following:

- *Fulfilling My Duty to God: For Aaronic Priesthood Holders*

- *For the Strength of Youth* pamphlet

- *Preach My Gospel* manual

- The Scouting program

The focus of this book is to help you use the tool of the Scouting program. In the next twelve chapters I will review some core purposes and principles, describe the Scouting program, share successful practices, warn of possible pitfalls, and encourage a paradigm shift.

Chapter 2: Bringing Young Men to Christ

As parents and Aaronic Priesthood leaders, your ultimate goal is to create conditions and provide opportunities to introduce young men to the pathway that leads to Christ. The prophet Moroni challenged each of us to "come unto Christ, and be perfected in him . . . " (Moroni 10:32).

As parents, you should be fully aware of what is happening in your son's quorum. Are you aware of the mutual theme for this year? Are you aware of what activities are planned for this month? Are spiritual elements included in your son's activities?

Elder David A. Bednar suggested that leaders plan and evaluate all activities and associations with young men through the following lens:

1. What are we doing to foster faith in Jesus Christ?

2. What are we doing to strengthen the family?

Elder Bednar further suggested that if our activities and associations do not foster faith in Christ or strengthen the family, we shouldn't be doing them.

This doesn't mean that all activities become lectures or firesides: it means that activities should be carefully planned with the goal that when the young man returns home he is incrementally closer to Christ and to his family. An increased effort and focus on planning and evaluating our activities in this way will bring us closer to the goal of bringing young men closer to Christ and of strengthening the family.

Are there traits, actions, or attitudes that let us know if a young man is "coming to Christ?" Is it possible to conduct an activity program with our youth they perceive as fun *and* that meets Elder Bednar's challenge?

The Young Men General Presidency and General Board accepted an assignment to answer three questions related to bringing young men to Christ, with the requirement that the answers must come from the scriptures. What follows is a summary of our study and prayer about these three important questions.

Question 1—How is it that young men come unto Christ?
Exercise faith . . . . Alma 32:27
Give place that a seed may be planted in his heart . . . . . Alma 32:28
Reflect and ponder about the good seed Alma 32:33–34
Nourish the word with diligence and patience . . . . . Alma 32: 41–42
Fast and pray . . . . Alma 5:46, Alma 17:3, Hel. 3:35
Search the scriptures. . . . . Alma 17:2, Hel. 3:29–30
Treasure up in his mind continually the words of life . . . D&C 84:85
Lay aside every sin . . . . Alma 7:15
Experience a lively sense of his own guilt . . . . Mosiah 2:38
Confess and forsake his sins . . . . D&C 58:43
Faithfully magnify his calling . . . . D&C 84:33–34

Here's a sample application of how these principles can be implemented in an Aaronic Priesthood quorum; of course, you would create your own themes tailored to your young men.

Lindon 18th Ward—Aaronic Priesthood Monthly Focus
January . . . . .Alma 32:27—Exercise Faith
February . . . . Alma 32:28—"Give place, that a seed may be planted in your heart"
March . . . . Alma 17:3—Fasting and Prayer
April . . . . Hel. 3:29–30—Search the Scriptures

- Have young men memorize the scripture for that month
- Emphasize the subject in bishop and bishopric interviews that month
- Insert the subject into quorum instruction
- Discuss the subject around the campfire on the monthly campout
- Have young men give sacrament meeting talks on the subject

Question 2—What is our role as leaders in helping young men come unto Christ?
Awaken them to a sense of their duty to God . . . . Alma 7:22
Teach by the Spirit of truth . . . . D&C 50:17, D&C 43:15
Walk in the Spirit. . . . . Gal. 5:16

Be led by the Spirit. . . . . 1 Ne. 4:6
Strengthen your brethren . . . . D&C 108:7
Learn your duty and act . . . . D&C 107:99
Let them see your good works . . . . Matt. 5:16
Search my sheep and seek them out . . . . Ezek. 34:11–12
Lead them into living fountains . . . . Rev. 7:17
Love the young man as your own soul 1 Sam.18:1
Esteem your brother as yourself . . . . D&C 38:24
Teach the doctrine of the kingdom. . . . . D&C 88:77
Teach with power and authority. . . . . Alma 17:3
Teach the principles of the gospel. . . . . D&C 42:12
Lead them in paths they have not known. . . . . .Isa. 42:16

Possible applications of these principles are varied. A few would include:

- Use the principles as a list of goals to help adult advisers assist young men.
- Use the principles as leadership training subjects for quorum presidencies.
- Prayerfully tailor a specific principle to a certain young man; each
  young man has different needs.

Question 3—How do we know a young man is coming unto Christ?

He will…
Press forward feasting upon the word of Christ . . . . 2 Ne. 31:20
Follow the example of the Son . . . . 2 Ne. 31:16
Do the things . . . that . . . his Redeemer would do . . . . 2 Ne. 31:17
Put off the natural man . . . . .Mosiah 3:19
Retain in remembrance the greatness of God . . . . .Mosiah 4:11
Call on the name of the Lord daily. . . . . .Mosiah 4:11
Have the image of God engraven upon his countenance . Alma 5:19
Have an eye single to the glory of God. . . . . D&C 4:5
Be in the service of his fellow beings. . . . . .Mosiah 2:17
Treasure up in his mind continually the words of life . . .D&C 84:85

Possible applications of these principles include:
- Evaluate each young man's progress using these guidelines.
- Use these principles in question format as springboards for discussion
  in bishop and bishopric interviews.
- Share these principles with the young man's parents; ask them to
  evaluate and monitor their son's progress.

Our job as parents and leaders is not to entertain; our goal is to bring boys to Christ. For parents this means that every family home evening, every family scripture study, and every family activity or vacation should be planned to include a spiritual dimension. For Aaronic Priesthood leaders it means that every combined activity, every activity night, and every camping trip should be planned with the goal of bringing young men closer to Christ. This can be accomplished by careful planning and by conducting a reflection at the conclusion of each activity. (You'll learn more about how to do this later.)

I recently spoke with a frustrated father who told me that his active seventeen- year-old son had not been on a campout for four years. "But," he said, "he's been to a lot of Utah Jazz games." The Young Men's adviser had season tickets, and they sat in box seats with all-you-can-eat catered food. After a few games the young men were not interested anymore. Entertainment is quickly forgotten, but meaningful activities leave imprints on minds and hearts that can last forever and influence future decisions.

In the summer of 2007 I spoke to 400 Scouts/deacons at Camp Hohobas in Washington state, in a beautiful setting overlooking the Hood Canal and the Olympic Mountains. I asked for two volunteers from the audience. I told them to act out a story related by Elder Carlos E. Asay as I read it to the audience. Hidden in a bag behind the podium I had a large Styrofoam sword and a small Styrofoam knife I had purchased at a toy store. I placed the two Deacons at opposite ends of the stage and read the following:

> As a small boy in grammar school, I had a teacher who made King Arthur and the knights of the Round Table come alive. She caused me to become so obsessed with stories of knights that I dreamed that I was one.
>
> One evening I dreamed that I was a knight on a white horse riding over the greens of England. Suddenly, without warning, a knight dressed in black armor and mounted on a black horse appeared at the edge of the forest. We measured each other carefully, lowered our lanced, and charged at full gallop. The lances struck target and both of us were knocked off our steeds.
>
> I scrambled to my feet knowing that swords would be drawn and that hand-to-hand combat was imminent. (at this point I threw the Styrofoam sword to the boy representing

the knight dressed in black). Fear gripped my heart as I saw my opponent rushing toward me flashing a long, gleaming sword (then I threw the small Styrofoam knife to the boy representing Elder Asay). Instinctively, I reached to my side and drew forth from the scabbard my weapon. That is when the dream turned into a nightmare! For in my hand was a small, dinky dagger – not a long, gleaming sword. I woke up in a cold sweat screaming for help.

Many times since that nightmarish experience, I have wondered about the serviceability of the Saints, particularly the young Latter-day Saints. When God calls you to serve, are you positioned in the scabbard and ready to be drawn? When the Lord draws you forth as his instrument in combating evil forces, what does he have in his hand – a long, gleaming sword or a dinky dagger?"

("The Message: Instruments of Righteousness," *New Era,* June 1983, 4)

The young man with the long gleaming sword prevailed. The young man with the dinky dagger was forced off the stage. With 400 young men fully engaged I asked them, "How are you prepared to face each day? If you forget to pray and read your scriptures, you face each day with the preparation of the dinky dagger. Satan will come at you each day with the long gleaming sword. He is always prepared. However, you can force Satan off the stage with your own sword of preparation. You are stronger than Satan; don't ever let him convince you otherwise."

This was a fun activity with a spiritual theme at a week-long Scout camp, and none of the 400 boys in attendance was daydreaming during the "sword fight" on the stage. With finely tuned spiritual antennas, Aaronic Priesthood leaders can "labor diligently to . . . persuade . . . our [young] brethren, to believe in Christ . . . " (2 Ne. 25:23). Aaronic Priesthood leaders working together with a strategic focus can help young men foster faith in Jesus Christ and empower them to "divide asunder all the cunning and the snares and the wiles of the devil . . ." (Hel. 3:29).

Pondering my responsibility toward those 400 young men led me to exclaim with Alma: "Behold, O Lord, their souls are precious, and many of them are our brethren; therefore, give unto us, O Lord, power and wisdom that we may bring these, our brethren, again unto thee" (Alma 31:35).

Chapter 3: Helping Young Men Develop a Testimony

As young men come unto Christ, they begin to feel the "swelling motions," the enlarged soul and enlightened understanding spoken of by Alma (Alma 32:28). Our goal as parents and Aaronic Priesthood leaders is to help young men develop testimonies of Christ and His Church. Our goal is to help them prepare for and live worthily to receive the Melchizedek Priesthood, receive the temple endowment, serve a faithful full-time mission and to become worthy husbands and fathers.

The family is the first institution charged with bringing young men to Christ; it is where the foundation of personal spiritual growth is built and nurtured. The Church, then, is the scaffolding that helps support and strengthen the family. The Aaronic Priesthood and Scouting are tools to help families with their young men. Working in harmony, the family and the Aaronic Priesthood should create an atmosphere where young men's individual testimonies can be nurtured and can flourish.

Elder M. Russell Ballard describes real testimony as something born of the Spirit and confirmed by the Holy Ghost—something that changes every aspect of our lives and that enables us to declare with humble clarity, "I know" (see M. Russell Ballard, "Pure Testimony," *Ensign,* Nov. 2004, 40).

Stephen E. Robinson adds the following:

> A testimony isn't like a hypothesis in science, which may be supported by the evidence one day and destroyed by it the next. It is a conviction *beyond* the available intellectual proof that some things are eternally true. The "provisionally converted" are those who have not received such a conviction (or who will not accept it) but who haven't found a good reason to leave—yet" (Stephen E.

Robinson, *Following Christ* [Salt Lake City: Deseret Book, 1995], 28–29).

How many of our young men can say, "I know"? Would it be safe to say that many of the young men in our Aaronic Priesthood quorums have not been "spiritually born of God" and are "provisionally converted"? This reality underscores the fragile spiritual condition of our young men.

The six years a young man spends in the Aaronic Priesthood program should be a spiritual training camp—complete with spiritually tuned parents and mentors, outdoor experiences, practical leadership experiences, twice-daily prayer, and daily readings of the playbook (scriptures). A comprehensive, spiritually focused Aaronic Priesthood experience can help young men recapture their elusive testimonies. On the other hand, an unstructured, casual approach—a focus on programs instead of people, a focus on checking off boxes instead of feeding their spirits—can contribute to the spiritual erosion of many young men.

These young men often find themselves in what President Monson describes as a growing pool of prospective elders. This pool is fed by a rushing river of Aaronic priesthood holders. Its outlet, however, is a mere trickle, because of the numbers of young men who are not advancing to the Melchizedek priesthood (see "The Priesthood—Mighty Army of the Lord," *Ensign*, May 1999, 48).

The Aaronic Priesthood pathway lies at a strategic junction in the spiritual journey of every man in the Church. Elder Bruce R. McConkie described it as "a preparatory priesthood, . . . the schooling ministry, which prepares its worthy and faithful ministers for the oath and covenant and perfection that appertain to the Melchizedek order" (Bruce R. McConkie, *Mormon Doctrine*, 11).

Each male member of the Church strives to be worthy to accept the five ordinances of salvation: baptism, confirmation, ordination to the Melchizedek Priesthood, endowment, and sealing. Each ordinance in the continuum builds on the previous ordinance, as represented below.

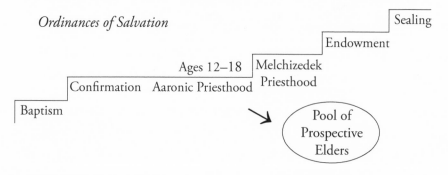

The Aaronic Priesthood experience should be a time of spiritual discovery for a young man, and a young man who bears the Aaronic Priesthood should have several encounters with the whisperings of the Holy Spirit, testifying of Christ. "… our personal life experiences become building blocks for our testimonies and add to our faith in the Lord Jesus Christ." (Elder Ronald A. Rasband, "Special Experiences," *Ensign*, May 2008, 11–12) The noble task of parents and adult advisers is to help create conditions and provide opportunities to introduce young men to the trail to testimony that leads them to Christ. Experiences in the outdoors can often create the conditions and provide opportunities for young men to strengthen their testimonies. One such experience was recited to me by an experienced Scoutmaster from California, "We were hiking in the Desolation Wilderness up to Susie Lake under a full moon (yes that was planned), and the Senior Patrol Leader/Deacons Quorum President was leading the group with the Assistant Scoutmaster and me bringing up the rear with the slower boys. One of those Sierra thunderheads appeared, and it started to rain. The 13 year old leader recognized the problem. He gathered the advanced group together and led them in prayer, invoking his Heavenly Father to stop the rain. The rain halted. I learned of this story several minutes later when we arrived at the destination and the boys told me about it. The story became a legend in our troop."

If we are focused on the spiritual welfare of our young men, we may be privileged to watch as many "cross the border of belief and enter the territory of testimony . . . a port of entry" (Elder Neal A. Maxwell, *Deposition of a Disciple* [Salt Lake City: Deseret Book Company, 1976], 51).

Chapter 4: Priesthood Keys

A foundational principle of a successful Aaronic Priesthood quorum and Scouting program is the proper use and recognition of priesthood keys. The exercise of priesthood authority in the Church is governed by those who hold priesthood keys (see D&C 65:2, 124:123). As stated in *Administering the Church,* those who hold priesthood keys have the right to preside over and direct the Church within a jurisdiction (see Book 2, 2010, 8).

The *LDS Scouting Handbook* makes it clear that quorum advisers are not to preside over meetings, but are to assist and advise those who do preside (see p. 3). A typical deacons or teachers quorum meeting includes a quorum president, two counselors, a secretary, two adult advisers, and a member of the bishopric. Who is presiding? The quorum president. The jurisdiction of a deacons quorum president includes all twelve- to thirteen-year-old young men residing in the ward; a teachers quorum president presides over all fourteen- to fifteen-year-old young men living in the ward; and the bishop, as president of the priests quorum, presides over all priest-age young men.

Would it be proper for a first counselor in a deacons quorum presidency conducting a quorum meeting to begin the meeting with the following? "Welcome to priesthood meeting. President Wilson [the deacons quorum president] is presiding, and he has asked that I, Brother Jones, conduct this meeting." It might sound a little unusual—but yes, it would be proper, and it follows the same pattern we typically follow in sacrament meeting, stake meetings and General Conference.

The Doctrine and Covenants says that deacons and teachers are to "invite all to come unto Christ" (D&C 20:59). This is done by the quorum president, who holds the authorized priesthood keys, assisted by his counselors and adult advisers. The adult role in the quorum is to honor the quorum president's priesthood keys by teaching and training the young men who have the right and responsibility to preside.

As a member of the Young Men General Board, I was asked to visit wards and observe Aaronic Priesthood meetings each week. As I visited wards and observed these quorums, I often saw in Priesthood meeting opening exercises the deacons quorum president, teachers quorum president, and an assistant to the priests quorum sitting in front with the bishopric, elders quorum president, and high priest group leader. This is a symbolic way to recognize priesthood keys. Another way to recognize those keys is to have the young men make the announcements in opening exercises. Doing this emphasizes their right and responsibility to exercise their priesthood keys.

In one ward visit I observed a bishop properly recognizing priesthood keys in an Aaronic Priesthood Committee meeting. The presidency of the Aaronic priesthood (the bishopric) in the ward was seated together. Directly across the room sat the deacons quorum president, the teachers quorum president, and a priest assistant. And on one side of the room sat the Young Men presidency and secretary (see the seating chart below).

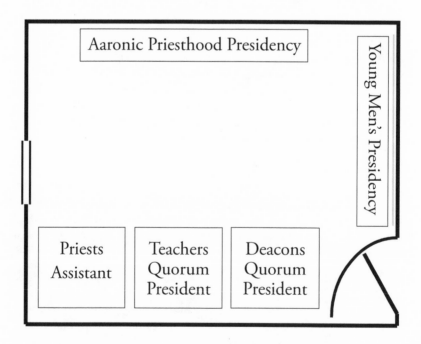

The seating arrangement was significant because the bishopric could look directly into the eyes of the young men. The other adults in the room were out of direct sight of those presiding and conducting.

As the meeting began, the bishop reminded the adults in the room that they were not to speak unless called on. A prayer was offered and the priest assistant gave a spiritual thought. An agenda was distributed to all present. The Young Men's secretary read the minutes from the last meeting. The bishop then asked each of the young men in turn to respond to assignments they had accepted the previous month. The teachers quorum president and the priest assistant gave home teaching reports for their quorums, name by name. Each quorum reported on their assignments to watch over the widows in the ward. The young men reported on visits to the widows during the past month to shovel snow, take out the trash, or move boxes. The deacons quorum president reported that his presidency had visited a new quorum member and his parents and had given them a Troop calendar, a Duty to God book, and the *For the Strength of Youth* pamphlet. The teachers quorum president reported back how he had prayerfully sought a solution for improving reverence in the quorum meeting. They then discussed the status of the Duty to God program and the Scouting program, and resolved a few calendaring issues. The bishop counseled the young men to always seek to strengthen the quorum by actively inviting the less active. The Young Men's president made a few comments, a prayer was offered, and the meeting was adjourned.

During the meeting the deacons and teachers quorum presidents were always addressed as "president," just as an elders quorum president would be. After the meeting I asked the young men's president what role he played in the preparation of this meeting. He told me he had met with the Priest Assistant; discussed assignments received the previous month, reminded him of some dates, and reassured him that he would do well in the meeting

President Henry B. Eyring told a story that illustrates the effect that a quorum presidency can have on the life of a boy when the presidency truly exercise their priesthood keys. In one of the wards in which President Eyring resided, a deacon lived near his home. That deacon was completely inactive; he had never participated with the other deacons in either a meeting or an activity. His mother, who was a member, did not attend church, and his stepfather did not belong to the Church.

One Sunday morning, the deacons quorum presidency discussed the deacon who never came, and the deacons quorum president assigned one of his counselors to go after the boy who was lost. That counselor, says President Eyring, was a shy young man—and President Eyring had some sense of how difficult that assignment would be. Yet the next Sunday there that counselor was, trudging up the hill past President Eyring's house to the home of the inactive deacon. About twenty minutes later, he came walking back down the hill, this time with the inactive deacon at his side. President Eyring watched the same scene repeat itself for a few more Sundays—and then the inactive deacon moved out of the ward.

Years later, President Eyring was approached by a gray-haired man who identified himself as the inactive deacon's grandfather. All those years later, that inactive deacon, now a grown man, remembered with fondness that experience—the first time he had felt recognized, cared for, and watched over by the shepherds of Israel (see Henry B. Eyring, "Watch with Me," *Ensign,* May 2001, 38).

Young men need to practice leadership in the Aaronic Priesthood, the preparatory priesthood. Priesthood keys, if properly recognized, can teach young men the joys and frustrations of serving and leading others. In a properly functioning quorum, youth leaders experience real-life experiences that can give them perspective to help them in future leadership positions.

Chapter 5: Shadow Leadership

In my weekly visits to Aaronic Priesthood quorums, I noticed a common tradition among many quorums. During the quorum meeting, the president stands and welcomes everyone. He often looks at the quorum adviser for prompting as to what to say next. Many times the quorum adviser will finish the quorum president's sentences. The young man generally has no written agenda in front of him and is "shooting from the hip." Often the quorum president asks the adviser, "What are we doing this week for our Young Men's activity?" This very common scenario is what I call "puppet leadership." In this case, the young man is simply the public extension of what the adult adviser knows.

Bishop Keith McMullin, second counselor in the Presiding Bishopric, said, "One way we could broaden the brotherhood and service aspects of the quorum is to put the quorum president in his proper role. We tend to empower the adviser in a deacons quorum with more authority than we do the quorum president." ("The Deacons Quorum," *Liahona*, Jan. 2005, 42). *Administering the Church* states, "The members of the Young Men presidency are quorum advisers, not quorum leaders.." (Book 2, 51)

In our Aaronic Priesthood quorums, we need to move from "puppet leadership" to "shadow leadership." Shadow leadership is more difficult for the adult adviser than puppet leadership, but it is the best way to teach a young man to learn and magnify his duty. In shadow leadership, the adult adviser should advise, remind, encourage, and train in private. The actors in the "public" performances (quorum meetings and presidency meetings) should be the young men. Bishop H. David Burton emphasized, "The adviser needs to develop the ability to be the "shadow leader" and somehow prompt the young men to perform their duties without the adviser becoming the effectual president of the quorum. Too often the quorum is a direct reflection of the current adviser." ("The Deacons Quorum," *Liahona,* Jan. 2005, 42).

If young men are to lead effectively, however, they need training. Leaders should meet with the youth presidency to go over the guidelines and rules, to discuss the realities of the budget, and to teach them how to plan with a purpose. A phone call reminder the night before can prevent many embarrassing situations, like the one I experienced recently. I was visiting a priests quorum, and we were sitting in the bishop's office waiting to start the quorum meeting. The bishop said that Brandon had been assigned to give the lesson this week—but Brandon wasn't there. He had accepted the assignment to teach several weeks earlier, but no one had followed up with him. The shadow leader needs to teach quorum presidencies how to follow up. The Priest quorum secretary in my ward makes phone calls each Saturday evening to the person assigned to teach the quorum lesson and those assigned to bless the sacrament. For the first few weeks, I had to call the Priest quorum secretary to remind him to remind the others, but he has now developed the habit. In addition, the Priest quorum assistant sends a text message to each quorum member the day before mutual to remind them of our activity.

By resisting the temptation to take over, good adult advisers allow young men to grow and to work towards being the next generation of Church leaders. President Harold B. Lee encouraged us as adult leaders to teach while remaining in the background—and then to let the youth do everything in their power (see N. Eldon Tanner, "Leading as the Savior Led," *New Era,* June 1977). Youth may make mistakes, but you will be able to help them learn from those mistakes and to build their confidence and skill. Well-trained youth will be able to plan effective meetings and activities and to help their quorum members face challenges, and your job is to gently guide them toward the correct decisions without taking over.

Provide each member of the presidency a small notebook that has his title displayed on the cover. Inside the notebook include a calendar, a roster of quorum members, and agendas for quorum and presidency meetings. Encourage each young man to bring the notebook to all meetings. It becomes a symbol of his calling.

Too often adult advisers ask young men to fulfill an assignment, but the assignment doesn't get written down. Experience has shown that assignments that aren't written down have a high probability of not getting done. Every time a young man conducts a meeting, he should have an agenda that has been prepared in advance. Helping young men learn to use an agenda is an important role for you as the adult adviser. When a well-prepared young man stands up to conduct a meeting, he may look at his adult adviser out of habit—but the adviser should simply give the young man an affirming nod. The young man will then look down at his agenda and will realize that he knows what to do.

Another key to shadow leadership is the division of responsibilities. Counselors in a presidency are rarely called on to do anything until the president is absent—and, as a result, many young men look at leadership as simply an honorary title that involves no real work. For more than twenty-five years, I have used a simple division of responsibilities sheet in every quorum or council I have worked in; here is a sample division of responsibilities for a priest quorum. If the young men have input into creating the division of responsibilities chart, and then are encouraged to fulfill their "Duty to God," the quorum will work.

Priest Quorum/Venturing Crew Division of Responsibilities

Bishop	Young Men President Quorum and Crew Adviser	Assistant (Youth)	Assistant Quorum and Crew Adviser	Assistant (Youth)	Secretary (Youth)
President of Quorum	Responsible for Aaronic Priesthood	Schedules presidency meetings	Responsible for mutual night	Maintains 3-month calendar, in charge of mutual	Keeps minutes of presidency meetings
Conducts semi-annual interviews	Shadow leader to youth leaders	Sacrament Coordinator	Shadow leader to youth leaders	Attends BYC	Service co-ordinator
Conducts bishopric youth committee (BYC)	Works closely with assistant	Attends presidency meetings	Works closely with assistant	Attends presidency meetings	Attends presidency meetings
Conducts Aaronic Priesthood Committee Meeting (APCM)	Attends BYC, APCM, presidency meeting	Activation Coordinator	Attends BYC, APCM, and presidency meeting	Reports for the quorum in opening exercises	Takes roll in quorum meetings
Attends ward Scouting committee meeting	Attends ward Scouting committee meeting	Attends APCM	Attends ward Scouting committee meeting	Correlates with Young Women on joint activities	Maintains active quorum roster
Presides at presidency meeting	Gives direction to quorum instruction	Rotates conducting quorum and presidency meetings	Helps with quorum instruction	Rotates conducting quorum and presidency meetings	Rotates conducting quorum and presidency meetings
		Coordinates missionary splits		Surveys adults for resources and youth for interests	

Shadow leadership is modeled in the scriptures. When the brother of Jared told the Lord that there was no light in the vessels, the Lord could have said, "Here are some rocks that I've touched to create light. Go put them in your boats." Instead, the Lord said, "What will ye that I should do that ye may have light in your vessels?" (Ether 2:23). The brother of Jared came up with the solution. He "went forth unto the mount . . . and did molten out of a rock sixteen small stones . . . and he did carry them . . . unto the Lord . . ." (Ether 3:1). Then he asked the Lord, "touch these stones, O Lord, with thy finger, and prepare them that they may shine forth in darkness . . ." (Ether 3:4). The brother of Jared was then blessed with a personal vision from the Lord.

A young man that learns to lead and take upon him the burdens of those he serves will strengthen his testimony as he sees the Lord's hand manifest in the lives of those people. He will see the Church in action, under the direction of the priesthood keys.

In our quorums and in our homes, are we practicing shadow leadership or puppet leadership? Are we empowering our sons or paving the way on an easy path? Never do for a young man what he can do for himself. We as adults should train youth how to lead, and then we should stand back. Young men should then preside and conduct quorum meetings and presidency meetings.

Chapter 6: The Activity Arm

With the purposes and principles firmly in place, let's describe the program adopted by the Church for the young men.

When was the last time you did a push-up? A proper push-up is a wonderful thing to behold. The back is straight and legs are together. The chest is the only part of the body that touches the ground, and both arms equally bear the weight of the body.

Think of a successful push-up as successfully bringing young men to Christ and strengthening their testimonies. One arm (the spiritual arm) is the Aaronic Priesthood; the other arm (the activity arm) is Scouting. Have you ever tried to do a push-up using only part of your strength in one arm—or, worse than that, a one-armed push-up? In strengthening boys, just as in strengthening biceps, using both arms is most effective.

In the April 2005 Aaronic Priesthood –Young Men General Conference Workshop Training, President Charles W. Dahlquist said, "It is very evident that in those stakes and wards where Scouting is used to strengthen the Priesthood, the young men of the Aaronic Priesthood are much stronger and better prepared than they would have been otherwise" (www.ldsscouting.org/Dahlquist.html).

Much of the corporate and academic world uses outcomes-based evaluation to measure productivity. At Brigham Young University, for example, each course is required to have program outcomes listed on the course outline. These outcomes look at impact, benefits, and changes to students as a result of completing the course.

The Aaronic Priesthood purposes are essentially crucial outcomes that will prepare young men to navigate successfully through life. If we taught a course entitled, "Preparing Young Men to be Spiritually Strong and Mighty Men" (see Alma 48:11), the program outcomes would be:

- Be converted to the gospel of Jesus Christ and live its teachings.

- Be able to serve faithfully in priesthood callings and fulfill the responsibilities of priesthood offices.

- Be willing to give meaningful service.

- Be prepared to live worthily to receive the Melchizedek Priesthood and temple ordinances.

- Be prepared to serve an honorable full-time mission.

- Be committed to obtain as much education as possible.

- Be prepared to become a worthy husband and father.

- Be committed to give proper respect to women, girls, and children. (*Administering the Church*, book 2, pg. 51)

Scouting, when properly applied, can be the laboratory to help meet these program outcomes. Meaningful Scouting activities plant the Aaronic Priesthood purposes deeply in the hearts of young men. Here are some ways that Scouting, the activity arm of the Aaronic Priesthood, helps fulfill each Aaronic Priesthood purpose:

- Become converted to the gospel of Jesus Christ and live its teachings. When Scouting is implemented properly, it provides rich and varied experiences where conversion can take place. It provides a laboratory for young men to test and experiment with gospel teachings.
- Serve faithfully in priesthood callings and fulfill the responsibilities of priesthood offices.
  In Scouting, young men are given specific assignments and responsibilities related to leadership, activities, and camping; by learning how to fulfill their Scouting responsibilities, young men are better able to fulfill the responsibilities of priesthood offices. In that way, Scouting can be a training ground for future Church leaders.
- Give meaningful service.
  Scouting requires service for advancement and teaches the need for a good turn daily. It provides the opportunity to serve in leadership positions and teaches a model of servant leadership.

- Prepare and live worthily to receive the Melchizedek Priesthood and temple ordinances.

  Scouting helps a young man come face-to-face with the reality of how congruent his life is with gospel teachings as he is placed in the care of a spiritually mature priesthood leader through whom the Spirit can work. A young man learns to make and keep oaths in Scouting in preparation to make and keep sacred covenants of the priesthood and in the temple.

- Prepare to serve an honorable full-time mission.

  A young man participating in ten years of Scouting with inspired and trained Cub Scout, Boy Scout, Varsity and Venturing leaders will have completed an effective missionary preparation program.

- Obtain as much education as possible.

  Scouting educates the mind and expands talents and skills through ranks and merit badge requirements. Most of the requirements in Scouting programs require a young man to read and to learn more about himself and the world around him. The Webelos activity badges and the merit badge program both introduce young men to hundreds of occupations and encourage young men to learn more about them.

- Prepare to become a worthy husband and father.

  When a young man learns and lives by the Scout Oath and Law, he will be a worthy husband and father.

- Give proper respect to women, girls, and children.

  One point of the Scout Law is to be courteous, and in the Scout Oath, young men pledge to help other people at all times.

Many of our wards are not fully utilizing Scouting as it was designed. Scouting should be a laboratory, not a lecture; purposeful, not casual; strategic, not haphazard; and spiritually strengthening, not merely entertaining.

The LDS Church adopts Scouting as four programs: Cub Scouting (ages eight through ten), Boy Scouting (ages eleven through thirteen), Varsity Scouting (ages fourteen and fifteen) and Venturing (ages sixteen through eighteen). The Boy Scouts of America allows the Church to tailor the programs to fit its needs. For example, in the Church young men are placed by age instead of academic grade, and leaders don't volunteer—

they are called. To maintain quorum identity and to recognize priesthood keys, each Aaronic Priesthood quorum has its own unit chartered to the Boy Scouts of America. The deacons quorum is a Boy Scout troop, the teachers quorum is a Varsity team, and the priests quorum is a Venturing crew.

The principal focus for the rest of this book is how rediscovering the spiritual dimensions of Scouting can help bring young men to Christ and strengthen individual testimonies.

Chapter 7: The Aims of Scouting

Any treatise on Scouting must include the aims of Scouting: character development, citizenship training, and mental and physical fitness (see *The Scoutmaster Handbook*, Boy Scouts of America, 1998, 7). The aims are the foundation for everything we do in Scouting. If a Scout leader is constantly aware of the Boy Scout aims, successful Scouting will happen.

Do the young men in the Church know the aims of Scouting? Do the parents and adult advisers in the Church know the aims of Scouting? Do they know that every Scouting activity should move Scouts toward these aims?

The boyhood of Jesus Christ was described in the scriptures in one verse, which captures the aims of Scouting amazingly well: "And Jesus increased in wisdom and stature, and in favour with God and man" (Luke 2:52). The phrase "favor with God" describes character; "favor with man" describes citizenship; and to increase "in wisdom and stature" describes mental and physical fitness.

Let's look at how the aims of Scouting are tied to exemplary men from the scriptures. In addition to these examples, think of ways you can incorporate the aims of Scouting into private conversations, family home evenings, father's interviews, discussions around a campfire, and informal discussions along the trail to testimony.

CHARACTER

Character is not easy to define—we know it when we see it, and we know when it is absent, but it can be difficult to put into words. "*Character* encompasses [our] personal qualities, values, and outlook" (*Scoutmaster Handbook*, 7). Horace Greeley exclaimed: "Fame is a vapor, popularity an accident, riches take wings, those who cheer today will curse tomorrow, only one thing endures—Character" (David Halberstam, *Breaks of the Game* [New York: Alfred A. Knopf, 1981).

A young man's character is manifest in his everyday habits and activities as well as in his relationships and dealings with others. The scriptures are filled with examples of character. One example is Nephi, who was traveling in the wilderness with his family toward the promised land. When he went hunting, broke his bow, and returned without food, his family suffered for the want of food, and they murmured. At one point even Nephi's father "began to murmur against the Lord his God" (1 Ne. 16:20).

But in the face of extreme adversity, Nephi could be counted on. He did not abandon his faith in God, even when his closest family members did. Nephi did not murmur; he "did make out of wood a bow, and out of a straight stick, an arrow. . . . And I said unto my father: Whither shall I go to obtain food?" (1 Ne. 16:23). Nephi demonstrated great character.

Nephi would have made a great Scout. Thanks to Dave Carlson from Seattle and Todd Moody from Las Vegas I share with you "Nephi Was An Eagle Scout".

If you read the Book of Mormon carefully, you will realize that Scouting was around long before Lord Baden Powell, and that Nephi probably earned enough merit badges to earn the rank of Eagle Scout.

He definitely earned the Camping merit badge. These were the requirements:

1. Pack up all of your gear, equipment and food.

2. Camp for eight years in the wilderness, sleeping each night under the sky or in a tent you have pitched.

3. Upon request, pack up your belongings and move to a new spot

Nephi earned the Hiking merit badge:

1. Hike from home for 3 days into the wilderness and establish a base camp.

2. Hike back home to pick up books you left behind.

3. Safely return to base camp with the books.

4. Hike home again and get other people for your trip.

5. Return to base camp with the other people, guiding them along the way.

6. Hike another 8 years in the wilderness, covering several hundred miles.

Archery merit badge:

1. Make a bow.

2. Make an arrow.

3. Hunt for food using the bow and arrow you made.

4. Kill sufficient game to feed you and 20 other people.

5. Perfect your archery skills to feed those people for several years.

Orienteering merit badge:

1. Obtain a compass that works according to the Spirit of God.

2. Follow the directions on the compass to find food, water and good camping spots.

3. When the compass stops working, convince the rest of your troop to exercise faith until it works again.

Public Speaking merit badge:

1. Speak in a public area in front of an angry crowd.

2. Tell the angry crowd about your dreams and convince some of those in the crowd to follow you.

3. Talk to the angry crowd about the books you enjoy reading.

4. Take other opportunities to speak to hostile audiences.

Salesmanship merit badge:

1. Offer to trade gold and silver for brass.

2. If you can't convince the other party to trade, offer something better.

3. Get deadly serious about your trade.

4. After the trade, find someone to carry the brass for you.

5. Convince a family and four beautiful young women to travel into the wilderness with you.

Family Life merit badge:

1. Travel with your entire family for at least eight years.

2. Obey your father in everything he asks, including things that seem impossible.

3. Forgive your siblings, even when they beat you with a rod, threaten to kill you and tie you to the mast of a ship.

4. Move to a new country with your family.

Metalwork merit badge:

1. Locate ore in a mountain.

2. Mine the ore.

3. Build a forge and bellows.

4. Work the ore in the forge and make useful tools.

5. Make plates from a high quality metal and write on those plates with a metal tool you have made.

Woodwork merit badge:

1. Locate trees useful to build objects.

2. Cut down those trees, remove the bark and saw into large boards.

3. Using the timber, make a large shelter or boat.

4. Coordinate the assistance of others with your various woodworking projects.

Sailing merit badge:

1. Build a sailing ship of sufficient size to carry you, your family and all your supplies.

2. Sail the ship across the ocean, safely navigating storms that occur as you travel.

3. Safely land the ship, your family and supplies in a new country.

Emergency Preparedness merit badge:

1. Gather a one year food supply.

2. Gather sufficient clothing, supplies and good for eight years of travel.

3. Learn to eat and survive on raw meat.

4. Collect, store and carry various grains and seeds.

Citizenship in the Nation merit badge:

1. Found a nation.

2. When the nation you have founded is threatened, move all of the people willing to follow you to a new location.

3. Found a new nation with the people who moved with you.

The development of character in young men is one of the primary goals of Scouting. Scouting encourages these young men to subscribe to an oath, law, motto, and slogan, and then provides opportunities for them to practice these values through small group associations and in outdoor settings. Leaders need to be sensitive to teaching moments both in formal meetings and in less formal outdoor settings. Many times the less formal settings provide rich opportunities to allow small failures to be character building experiences. Here is a recent dialogue observed on a Scouting internet chat site:

Jon from Georgia, "Some people think we should coddle and micromanage the youth until they are 18, and then shove them out to West Bukavania and expect them to be effective missionaries. And they should do this without ever having experienced the joy of defeat and the blessing of failure when they were young and issues weren't life changing.

Dil from Arizona, "I think you are correct, some of life's best lessons (and best Scout outings) were when: the food got left home (and the Scoutmaster knew this but could not get the boys to check the list just one more time before we leave).

The boys unpacked the tent and found out that there were no poles.

It rained and only the Scoutmaster had a rain coat.

When the skunks came into camp because 'someone didn't properly put up the extra food', and therefore no breakfast the next morning- the skunks ate it in front of the boys."

Bob from New Hampshire, "I think you left out the best one. After lugging all the canned food the mile into the campsite and building a nice fire to cook it on, the Scouts realized that no one had brought a can opener. The hours listening to them brainstorm ways to open a can and then watch them try them out for hours until one of them realized that their knife had a can opener thing on it. Priceless."

Mark from Utah, "After agonizing about the same problems, my boys figured out my knife must have a can opener (none of theirs did). Looking back, it wasn't very kind, but when they came to ask me if they could use it, I "rented" it to them for the price of some tasty snacks they had carried in."

CITIZENSHIP

According to *Webster's Dictionary*, a *citizen* is "a member of a state or nation who owes allegiance to it by birth or naturalization and is entitled to certain rights," such as the right to vote. The suffix *ship* is "the quality or state of being" (*Webster's New World Dictionary* [New York: Simon & Schuster, 2003], 120, 592). Citizenship implies action.

The twelfth Article of Faith states, "We believe in being subject to kings, presidents, rulers, and magistrates, in obeying, honoring, and sustaining the law" (Articles of Faith 1:12). In addition, *The Family: A Proclamation to the World* says that parents have a responsibility to teach their children to be law-abiding citizens wherever they live.

One of the best examples of citizenship in the scriptures is Captain Moroni. He was the ultimate Boy Scout. His "soul did joy in the liberty and the freedom of his country . . . [He was] a man who did labor exceedingly for the welfare and safety of his people. . . . and he had sworn with an oath to defend his people, his rights, and his country, and his religion, even to the loss of his blood" (Alma 48:11–13).

Compare and contrast Captain Moroni with Amalickiah, his opponent on the battlefield:

Captain Moroni	Amalickiah
- Strong and mighty man (see Alma 48:11)	- Large and strong man (see Alma 46:3)
- Prayed for liberty and freedom (see Alma 46:13,16)	- Sought to destroy liberty (see Alma 46:10)
- Stirred Nephites to patriotism (see Alma 46:19–22)	- Stirred Lamanites to anger (see Alma 47:1)
- Appointed by the voice of the people (see Alma 46:34)	- Gained power by fraud and deceit (see Alma 48:7)
- People ran to support the cause (see Alma 46:21)	- People were doubtful concerning the cause (see Alma 46:29)

The Book of Mormon states that "if all men had been, and were, and ever would be, like unto Moroni, behold, the very powers of hell would have been shaken forever; yea, the devil would never have power over the hearts of the children of men" (Alma 48:17).

Those are the kind of citizens we want our young men to be!

The development of participating citizens is one of the primary goals of Scouting. The Scouting program itself helps young men practice good citizenship by participating in a troop governed by rules based on the common good. Three required merit badges in Scouting address citizenship; additional merit badges related to Citizenship include:

- American Cultures

- American Heritage

- Crime Prevention

- Disabilities Awareness

- Emergency Preparedness

- Family Life

FITNESS

The word *fit* means "to be suitable to . . . suited to some purpose, function, . . . proper; right, . . . healthy." The suffix *ness* "is the state, quality, or instance of being" (*Webster's New World Dictionary* [New York: Simon & Schuster, 2003], 246, 433). Fitness, then, is the quality of being suitable. In Scouting, fitness means to be suitable spiritually, mentally, and physically. President Ezra Taft Benson wrote that often we think of *fitness* only in terms of physical fitness—but that true fitness involves mental, emotional, and spiritual fitness as well, the reason why we challenge Scouts to be "physically strong, mentally awake, and morally straight" (see "Scouting Builds Men," *New Era*, February 1975, 14).

Not surprisingly, Scouting teaches the same code of physical health as the Church, and all Scouting literature validates the principles taught by the Church in the Word of Wisdom.

Scouting teaches young people to get the most out of life by being mentally and physically fit. The Cub Scouts sports program, many Boy Scout merit badges, and the Venturing Quest award are all focused on physical fitness. Scouting also encourages spiritual fitness on its application for membership, in the oath and law, through its religious awards, and with its emphasis on using the outdoors to strengthen faith. The Scout *Constitution* states: "The Boy Scouts of America maintains that no boy can grow into the best kind of citizen without recognizing his obligation to God" (William D. Murray, *The History of the Boy Scouts of America* [New York: Boy Scouts of America, 1937], 499).

When you compare the aims of Scouting to the purposes of the Aaronic Priesthood, there is obvious harmony. But this connection between the two won't be clear unless we explicitly incorporate the aims of Scouting into our local Scouting program. An email I received from an LDS Scouter in Florida expressed this idea quite well:

> We have so very few trained leaders in this area, and it is often reflected in the quality of the program. The Young Men leaders' hearts are in the right place; they love our boys, and our boys love them. But the leaders often struggle unnecessarily because they don't know and understand the aims and methods of the program.

The aims of Scouting create the foundation for the methods/strategies of Scouting. Commit the aims of Scouting to memory, and use them as a measurement of all you do in Scouting. In addition to Elder Bednar's challenge, ask the following question when planning activities: "What are we doing in this activity that promotes character, citizenship, and fitness?"

Chapter 8: The Methods/Strategies of Scouting

At each level, Scouting has created methods or strategies to achieve its aims; over time, these methods have created a fertile learning environment and have contributed to growth in young people. If emphasized and mastered, the methods will develop the aims of character, citizenship, and fitness in our young men and will help them become closer to Christ.

The chart below shows the consistencies and the strategic progression from dependence to interdependence (from left to right) in the methods as boys progress from Cub Scouting to Venturing. The ideals are consistent in all four programs. Advancement is a key strategy in Cub Scouting, Boy Scouting, and Varsity Scouting, and then advancement evolves into recognition in Venturing. Young men progress from a den to a patrol, then to a team, and then to group activities. For example, see the progression from activities that are centered in the home and neighborhood (Cub Scouting), to activities that are centered in the outdoors (Boy Scouting and Varsity Scouting), to high-adventure activities (Venturing). As another example, look at the progression from family involvement to adult association. Leadership is first introduced as a method in Boy Scouting. Notice the absence of the uniform method and the addition of the teaching others method in Venturing.

Cub Scouting	Boy Scouting	Varsity	Venturing
Ages 8-10	Ages 11-13	Ages 14-15	Ages 16-18
The Ideals	Scouting Ideals	Scouting Ideals	The Ideals
Den	Patrol	Squad/Team	Group Activities
Advancement	Advancement	Advancement	Recognition
Family	Adult Association	Adult Association	Adult Association
Activities	Outdoor	Outdoor	High Adventure

Cub Scouting	Boy Scouting	Varsity	Venturing
Uniform	Uniform	Uniform	
Neighborhood	Personal Growth	Personal Growth	Teaching Others
Character Connections	Leadership	Leadership	Leadership

Another way to look at the methods is by acronyms. I have committed the methods to memory by creating the following acronyms, which take the first letter of each method and organize them into a boy's name.

Cub Scouting Methods	Dan A. Cuft
Boy Scouting Methods	Paul Soap
Varsity Scouting Methods	Saul Soap
Venturing Methods	Al Right

CUB SCOUTING METHODS

Let me introduce you to Dan A. Cuft. Dan is a Cub Scout. In the LDS Church, Cub Scouting serves boys ages eight through ten in a Cub Scout pack. For Dan to receive the total benefits of Cub Scouting (character, citizenship, and Fitness), to draw closer to Christ, and to strengthen his testimony, he must have a program where each Cub Scout method is utilized.

Den	Boys need and want to belong to a group. The den is the place where belonging is created through practicing skills, exploring interests, learning values, and forming friendships. In the den, boys are given opportunities to work with others, to do their best, and to have fun. Many boys experience leadership for the first time by serving as denners and assistant denners.
	A Den Leader in Utah shared with me the following:
	I have watched boys that were considered behavior problems join our den and within a short time develop character traits of a respectable young man that can still have fun. We continue to teach them how to develop good character traits by using the 12 core characteristics of cub scouting. We've given our denner more responsibilities and

that has been truly amazing to watch the changes in the Cub Scouts when we do that. We have watched the boys gain stronger testimonies of the Gospel, of service and prayer.

My mother was a den leader for ten years. She had four sons spaced in such a way so that when one of us would graduate into Boy Scouts, another one would enter Cub Scouting. She wanted to be our den leader. Some of the fondest memories of my childhood came from the den meetings held in our home. For the first time in my life I was in a small group where I could build close friendships and be noticed for my talents more readily. My class at school was too large and too formal to provide these kinds of opportunities.

Advancement

Advancement is another one of the methods used to achieve Scouting's aims. Everything a Cub Scout does to advance is designed to achieve these aims and aid in his personal growth. The advancement plan provides fun and challenging experiences by helping boys gain self-motivation and a sense of personal achievement while strengthening family relationships. Remember, though, that the badges are a means to an end— not an end in themselves. Positive recognition is important to young boys.   I remember as a Cub Scout earning so many arrow points that when I tucked my shirt tails in my pants, some of the arrows disappeared. So I untucked my shirt just enough so everyone could see all the arrow points I had earned.

Neighborhood

Boys are connected to their neighborhoods and communities through their activities and service. In turn, the community gives them a sense of purpose, worth, and belonging.

A Cub Scout den should "capture" the imagination and energy of boys in a neighborhood. My mother invited the boys in our neighborhood who were not members of the Church to join our den, and most of them did! It was a structured "play group" that built self-esteem, provided wholesome entertainment, planted many gospel seeds, and brought our neighborhood closer together.

Activities

Boys participate in a variety of den and pack activities, such as games, projects, skits, songs, outdoor activities, and service experiences. Cub Scout activity programs provide opportunities for growth in character development, citizenship training, and physical fitness.

Character Connections

In the Cub Scout program, leaders learn to identify and utilize character lessons in activities so that boys can learn to know, commit, and practice the twelve core values of Cub Scouting— citizenship, compassion, cooperation, courage, faith, health and fitness, honesty, perseverance, positive attitude, resourcefulness, respect, and responsibility. Many achievements and electives in the Wolf, Bear, and Webelos books have a know, commit, and practice section.

Uniform

The Cub Scout uniform helps build pride, loyalty, and self-respect. Wearing the uniform encourages a neat appearance, a sense of belonging, and a shared identity for both the boys and the leaders.

One of my favorite things to do as a professional Scouter was to conduct a uniform inspection for a Cub Scout pack. The boys lined up at attention, and the parents looked on in either horror or pride, depending on how their son looked. Rich or poor, the boys looked the same and were proud to be associated with each other.

Family	Family involvement is an essential part of Cub Scouting, and parents provide leadership, support, and resources. Active family participation ensures that boys have a successful experience in Cub Scouting. Most of the Cub Scout achievements and electives should be completed at home.
The Ideals	Practices such as the Cub Scout Promise, the Law of the Pack, and the Cub Scout sign, handshake, motto, and salute help reinforce values taught at home and at Church. Every den and pack meeting should begin with the Cub Scout sign and promise.

In the LDS Church, the Primary organization oversees Cub Scouting. *Administering the Church* manual states: "Cub Scouting activities take the place of activity days for boys ages 8 through 11. To maintain a gospel focus in Scout activities, leaders use the *Faith in God for Boys* guidebook as one of their resources. As boys fulfill requirements in the guidebook, they also qualify for religious awards in Scouting." (Book 2,92)

BOY SCOUTING METHODS
Now let me introduce you to Paul Soap. In the LDS Church, Boy Scouting serves boys ages eleven to thirteen in a Boy Scout troop. The eleven-year-old boys are in a patrol that meets separately from the troop under the direction of the Primary organization. The twelve- to thirteen-year-old boys are Boy Scouts—as well as deacons in the Aaronic Priesthood. Too often Boy Scouting is reduced to nothing more than earning badges and checking off boxes. For Paul Soap to receive the total benefits of Boy Scouting (character, citizenship, and fitness), to draw closer to Christ, and to strengthen his testimony, he must help plan a program where each Boy Scout method is utilized.

Patrol Method	Empowering boys to be leaders is the core of Scouting, and the patrol method is a form of shadow leadership (discussed in Chapter 5). The patrol method is the foundation to a successful troop, as these quotes illustrate:

> The patrol method is not ONE method in which Scouting can be carried on. It is the ONLY method (Roland Phillips, as quoted in *Handbook for Scoutmasters: A Manual for Leadership*, Vol. 1, 3rd edition [Boy Scouts of America, 1938], 161).

> Within the larger community of the troop, the patrol is a Scout's "family circle." . . . Each patrol helps its members develop a sense of pride and identity. The boys . . . divide up the jobs to be done, and share in the satisfaction of accepting and fulfilling group responsibilities (*The Scoutmaster Handbook* [Boy Scouts of America, 2007], 8).

> *Train 'em, trust 'em, and let 'em lead!* (*Handbook for Scoutmasters: A Manual for Leadership*, Vol. 1, 3rd edition Boy Scouts of America, 1938), 224).

Lord Robert Baden-Powell, the founder of Scouting, stated that the main object of the patrol system is:

> . . . to give real responsibility to as many boys as possible with a view to developing their characters. If the Scoutmaster gives his Patrol Leader real power, expects a great deal from him and leaves him a free hand in carrying out his work, he will have done more for that boy's character expansion than any amount of school training could ever do (Robert Baden-Powell, *Baden-Powell's Scouting For Boys* [London: C. Arthur Pearson Ltd., 1944], 53).

THE EASY CHAIR CHALLENGE

"An old experienced Scoutmaster said once, 'The test of the Patrol Method is in the easy chair!'" Here's what he meant:

> Get an easy chair and place it in a corner of the Troop meeting room. If you can sink into it just after the opening ceremony and just *sit* throughout the meeting, without a worry for its success, without lifting a finger or moving a foot until the time comes for the closing— well, then your Troop is run on the Patrol Method—your boy leaders are actually *leading (Handbook for Scoutmasters: A Manual for Leadership,* Vol. 1, 3rd edition [Boy Scouts of America, 1938], 168).

I served as a Boy Scout camp director for four summers in California and Colorado. I saw many Scoutmasters who brought their favorite easy chair and a book to read for the week. They didn't follow the boys around camp and make sure that each one was where he was supposed to be. They weren't stressed or overly anxious. The senior patrol leader and the patrol leaders ran the troop, while the Scoutmaster gave advice and counsel from his easy chair. The troop ran well at camp because it was an extension of how the troop ran back at home.

Too often the LDS unit at summer camp is a combination of Scouts, Varsity and Venturing thrown together the week before camp and supervised by different dads each day, instead of consistent adult supervision all week long. This is not the patrol method.

Advancement

Advancement is one of the eight methods used

by Scout leaders to help boys fulfill the aims of the Boy Scouts of America. Properly used, a troop's advancement program can tie together and energize the other seven methods. According to *The Scoutmaster Handbook* (p. 123), four basic steps lead to Boy Scout advancement:

1. A Scout learns
2. A Scout is tested
3. A Scout is reviewed
4. A Scout is recognized

My oldest son once returned home from Young Men's activity night and announced that he had earned the Woodworking merit badge. He said that the Scout leaders brought partially assembled bird houses and gave a lecture on working with wood. The boys finished assembling the bird houses and got their merit badge cards signed. In that process, though, my son was not tested or reviewed.

Often the only measurement we use for success in Scouting is the number of Eagle badges awarded. And sometimes in our zeal to produce Eagle Scouts, we take shortcuts in the advancement process. If done properly and if done using the four steps of advancement, the process of becoming an Eagle Scout can leave lasting memories and can build a foundation for adulthood.

A fifty-three year old LDS Scout leader remembers the following experience vividly:

> On a campout with my troop forty years ago, I asked my Scoutmaster to sign off my first Scout breakfast, and was taken back when he asked to come and see it. I thought all I had to do was tell him I'd done it and he would sign off.

We walked from his cooking fire to mine, and after surveying a scrambled pancake (how could I put butter on the pan before pouring the batter, when I didn't bring any?) and my "slab" of fried spam (so thick that it was still frozen on the inside), he asked "Did you do your best?" I told him I had met the requirements—I had cooked a breakfast and would eat it. He asked, "Would I be doing my best as a Scoutmaster if I signed you off on this?" I admitted he wouldn't, and was deeply disappointed that I wouldn't be getting my second-class rank at the next court of honor.

At the next month's campout I proudly asked my Scoutmaster to come to my cooking fire, where we dined on pancakes that didn't stick in my mess kit. They had blueberries in them that I had packed frozen and let thaw overnight so they would be perfect at breakfast. The spam was replaced by Jimmy Dean sausages. Thanks to my Scoutmaster, I learned that doing my best was worth the time that it might take, and that just getting by was not the way I wanted to live my life.

Several years ago a young man came to my home to ask advice about an Eagle Project. I asked him why he wanted to be an Eagle Scout. He replied without hesitation, "So I can drive." Sometimes in our zeal to produce Eagle Scouts we provide incentives that become more important than the award. One leader commented that the goal of Scouting is *not* to make sure that every boy becomes an Eagle or that the troop become the top one in the Church. The only goal, he said, was to develop boys that would return to Heavenly Father with the strongest character and the best spirit (see Ruel A. Allred, *New Era,* Feb. 1978).

As one of the eight methods of Scouting, advancement is a natural outcome of the other seven, according to *The Scoutmaster Handbook.* "A boy whose Scouting experience is introducing him to the BSA ideals, the patrol method, the outdoors, association with adults, personal growth, leadership development, and the uniform will almost certainly find himself moving steadily along the BSA's advancement trail" *(The Scoutmaster Handbook* [Boy Scouts of America, 2002], 8).

I often observe Boy Scout troops out of balance, emphasizing the method of advancement at the expense of the other seven methods. In some troops, Scouts are advancing with few campouts, little emphasis on uniform, no patrol method in place, and little Scout spirit. Many troops are simply advancement machines with all effort expended for one result—and too often most of the effort is exerted by the leaders and parents, not the boys.

Think about it: What's the first question you ask your son when he returns from a week of Scout camp? If you're like many parents, you ask, "How many merit badges did you earn?" Each of us could think of at least ten other questions that are more important and have greater eternal consequence. Don't get me wrong—I'm not suggesting that we deemphasize advancement. I'm only suggesting that we balance our troop with an emphasis on all eight methods.

We want our young men to "become" Eagle Scouts, not just get their Eagle awards. We want them to "receive" their endowment, not just take out their endowment. We want them to "become" a missionary, not just go on a mission.

Uniform

The uniform reinforces the fact that all members of the Boy Scouts of America are equal to one another. There are other advantages to the uniform as well. Wearing the uniform helps develop a sense of belonging to the patrol and troop. It makes a statement to others, too—people seeing a boy in a Scout uniform expect someone of good character who is prepared to help those around him. The uniform is just as important for Scout leaders, who should set the example.

Many successful troops wear a casual uniform (a screen-printed polo or tee shirt) on activity nights and campouts, and reserve the formal uniform for Courts of Honor. The key is to wear something that ties the whole group together. If the young men feel ownership, they will most likely wear the uniform.

Leadership

One of the hallmarks of the Boy Scouts of America is the excellent leadership training it provides for youth leaders. Learning how to lead is a critical component in a young man's journey on the pathway to Christ. A young man needs to learn from experience how to be a Christ-like leader—a servant leader. The stage for practicing leadership is in the Aaronic Priesthood quorums and Scouting. Unfortunately, most young men receive little or no training when first called to serve in an Aaronic Priesthood quorum.

One important place for the boy to practice leadership skills is the patrol leaders' council. According to *The Patrol Leader Handbook*, "The patrol leaders' council plans the yearly troop program at the annual program planning conference. It then meets monthly to fine-tune the plans for the upcoming month"

("Patrol Leader," www.scouting.org/BoyScouts/PatrolLeader.aspx).

The National Council of the Boy Scouts of America has created National Youth Leadership Training (NYLT) for Boy Scout and Varsity-age youth, and the Venturing Leadership Skills Course (VLSC) and Kodiak for Venturers. The NYLT may have a different name in your council, but the format is the same. Young men go to an outdoor setting for a week to learn leadership skills and to have the opportunity to apply them. During the week the young men go through a virtual experience of one month in the life of a troop—each day at camp is a week in the life of a troop. Each participant learns about the patrol leaders' council, how to run troop meetings, and how to teach. At the end of the week the trainees participate in an outdoor event to apply the skills they have learned. Each leadership skill has an application.

I met Nathan Foster, a nineteen-year-old from Boise, Idaho, at Camp Bradley in the Sawtooth Mountains of Idaho. Nathan was serving on the Camp Bradley waterfront staff and shared with me his experience with NYLT—an experience that had given him the confidence he needed to teach in the mission field:

> "If it wasn't for NYLT, I wouldn't be going on a mission. Before I went to NYLT I was not headed in the right direction. The skills I learned, the brotherhood I shared, the goals I made at NYLT all gave me confidence and direction at a critical time in my life. I learned to make S.M.A.R.T. goals: Specific, Measurable,

Attainable, Relevant, and Timely. Before NYLT I was drifting, not really getting anywhere. I served on staff for NYLT. The goals I set were Scouting goals, troop goals, and personal goals. One of the personal goals I set was to serve a mission. The combination of being in an outdoor setting with quality people and setting goals changed the focus of my life. The skills and confidence I learned in NYLT will help me be a better teacher as a missionary. I learned that to teach effectively you must teach at the learner's level. I practiced my teaching techniques with a non-member on the NYLT staff and gave him a Book of Mormon.

Soon after we talked, Nathan received his mission call to the Florida Tampa Mission.

Scouting Ideals

The ideals of Boy Scouting—ideals that lead to what's called the "Scout spirit"—are spelled out in the Scout Oath, Scout Law, Scout Motto, and Scout Slogan. Repeating these at Scout meetings and activities reinforces the ideals of Scouting.

Do you believe that repetition brings conviction? Does reciting a scripture or an oath over and over again make a difference in behavior? Several years ago I was asked to speak about Scouting to the Rotary Club in Newport, Oregon. I began the speech by making the Scout sign and saying, "A Scout is Trustworthy, Loyal, Helpful, Friendly. . . ." And then I stopped. The eighty Rotarians in the room finished the Scout Law in a unified chorus. I called on an elderly gentleman to tell me when he last recited the Scout Law. With tears welling up in his eyes he said, "About fifty years ago."

I'm convinced that a moral compass and guidepost is created when young men frequently recite the Scout Oath, Law, Motto, and Slogan, and then engage in regular discussions about them.

On the side of the dusty gravel road leading into Treasure Mountain Scout camp in Wyoming—in the shadows of the Grand Teton, with their lush aspens and pines—visitors are greeted with three six-foot-high engraved wooden posts. The white letters against the dark brown wood on the first post spell out "God and Country." One hundred feet down the road another post is engraved with "Other People." The last sign says simply, "Self." These posts offer a graphic reminder of the priority professed by those who call themselves Scouts. First we promise to do our best to do our duty to (1) God, then (2) our country. Next we promise to obey the Scout Law, to (3) help other people at all times, then to (4) keep ourselves physically strong, mentally awake, and morally straight.

All oaths in the Boy Scouts of America have the same order of priorities.

Cub Scout Promise	Boy Scout Oath	Venturing Oath
I, (name) promise to do my best to do my **duty to God** and my **country**, to help **other people** and to obey the Law of the Pack. (*Cub Scout Wolf Handbook*, 17).	On my honor I will do my best to do my **duty to God** and my **country** and to obey the Scout Law; to help **other people** at all times; to keep **myself** physically strong, mentally awake, and morally straight (*The Boy Scout Handbook* America, 1998). [Boy Scouts of America, 1998], 9).	As a Venturer, I promise to do my **duty to God** and help strengthen America, to help others, and to seek truth, fairness, and adventure in our world (*Venturing Leader Manual,* Boy Scouts of America, 1998).

Do our Aaronic Priesthood young men understand this priority? Do we recite the Scout Oath and Law at every meeting? Do we discuss it and dissect it to help young men assimilate it in their lives?

The Crossroads of America Council in Indianapolis conducts "Lunch on the Circle" each year. In the center of Indianapolis on the third Thursday of June, adult volunteers and Scouts in uniform serve lunch to employees of the downtown businesses. The money raised ($25,000) creates "camperships" that help needy young men go to summer camp by paying half the summer camp fee. The recipients of the camperships are asked to help serve the food. As I was going through the food line, I asked one of the sharply dressed young men to tell me about his troop. Then I asked him if he knew the Scout Slogan. He responded without hesitation, "Do a good turn daily." I asked him next about the Scout Motto. "Be prepared!" he said. The Scout Law? He repeated the twelve points enthusiastically. We want young men like this Indianapolis Scout, with the ideals of Scouting assimilated in their souls.

The Scout Law in the Scriptures

In the fall of 2003, an instructor in the Missionary Training Center gave his missionaries an unusual assignment: find scriptures that correlate with the twelve points of the Scout Law. Here's what the missionaries reported back:

Trustworthy
Helaman 10:1–4, 11–12—"unwearingness."
Loyal
Job 1:21—"the Lord gave, and the Lord hath taken away; blessed be the name of the Lord."
Helpful
Luke 10:30, 33–34—Samaritans were helpful

even though they were hated and despised by the Jews.

Friendly
John 4:5–30—The women at the well was a Samaritan, and Jesus was friendly to her.

Courteous
Luke 17:11–19—Ten lepers were healed physically, and one was "made whole." The leper that returned was a Samaritan. Swift gratitude is the sweetest.

Kind
I Kings 17:10–12—Widow helps Elijah.

Obedient
Alma 56:47–48, 57:21—"exactness."

Cheerful
John 16:33—"Be of good cheer."

Thrifty
Ruth 2:15–17—Ruth gleaned in the field.

Brave
Alma 46:10–13—Captain Moroni raised the title of liberty.

Clean
Mosiah 4:30—Genesis 39:7–15

Reverent
Ether 3:1–5—The brother of Jared approaches the Lord.

There are twelve points to the Scout Law and twelve months in a year. A ward Young Men's program could adopt one point of the Scout Law each month. Each young man could be assigned to bring a scripture on the monthly campout to illustrate that month's point of the Scout Law. This plan would help parents and boys get together before the campout to prepare a scripture in addition to gathering the necessary camping supplies. The spiritual dimension of Scouting must dominate all that we do. President Spencer W. Kimball pointed out that Scouting can change the course of a boy's life by committing him to do his best and by using the Scout principles to help him forge a lasting companionship with his Heavenly Father (see *Ensign,* May, 1977).

Outdoors

The Scoutmaster Handbook emphasizes that much of Scouting is designed to take place outdoors in settings that provide real adventure—and that the most successful troops are those with a strong outdoor program.

A Scoutmaster in Logan, Utah, related to me that during his third year as Scoutmaster he was camping in Logan Canyon with his troop. It was twenty degrees below zero. He lay there shivering in his tent, wondering why the Lord wanted him to go camping. That was the beginning of his search as to why outdoor experiences are so important to the Lord. He started to search the scriptures to find cases where the Lord had sent his prophets and his people out into the wilderness.

He found that Moses and his people went on a forty-year camping trip that prepared them to enter the promised land. Adam was sent out of the garden into the wilderness to gain experience, and Abraham left his home and became the father of all nations. Zion's Camp and the Mormon Battalion prepared future Church leaders.

After searching the scriptures, this Scoutmaster changed his attitude. He realized that just being out in the campsites, cooking together, serving each other, and learning together can create opportunities to positively influence young men. In both the classroom and at the campsite, Scouts learn to serve and love their quorum members.

Inspired by this Scoutmaster's revelation, I searched the scriptures and had a similar experience. Here are my findings:

• Abraham was commanded to "Take now thy son, thine only son Isaac . . . into the land of Moriah . . . upon one of the mountains which I will tell thee of" (Gen. 22:2).

• "So Moses brought Israel from the Red sea, and they went out into the wilderness . . . "(Ex. 15:22) as the Lord commanded.

• ". . . and the LORD called Moses up to the top of the mount . . ." (Ex. 19:20) to receive the tablets containing the Ten Commandments.

• When the prophet Elijah pronounced a famine on the land, the Lord sent him to "hide thyself by the brook Cherith . . ." (1 Kgs. 17:3).

• When Naaman came to the prophet Elisha to be healed of leprosy, he was told to "Go and wash in Jordan seven times . . . " (2 Kgs. 5:10).

• Lehi was commanded in a dream that "he should take his family and depart into the wilderness" (1 Ne. 2:2) to save his people from destruction.

• Enos went to hunt in the forest and "kneeled down before my Maker, and I cried unto him in mighty prayer . . . " (Enos 1:4).

• Alma fled into the wilderness, hid near the water in a "thicket of small trees" (Mosiah 18:5), repented of his sins, and taught and baptized those who believed on his words.

• When Joseph Smith "came to the conclusion that I must either remain in darkness and confusion, or else I must do as James directs, that is, ask of God. . . . I retired to the woods to make the attempt" (JS–History 1:13–14).

- When the Saints in this dispensation needed to separate themselves from persecution, they went to the wilderness— the American West.
- ". . . the word of God came unto John . . . in the wilderness. And he came unto all the country about Jordan, preaching the baptism of repentance for the remission of sins" (Luke 3:2–3).
- When Christ needed to prepare for his ministry, he was "led up of the Spirit into the wilderness . . ." (Matt. 4:1).
- During His ministry when Christ was pressed by great multitudes, "he withdrew himself into the wilderness, and prayed" (Luke 5:15–16).
- ". . . Jesus taketh Peter, James, and John . . . and bringeth them up into an high mountain apart, And was transfigured before them . . ." (Matt.17:1–2).
- When Christ was fulfilling his ministry and the ultimate Atonement, "he came out, and went, as he was wont, to the mount of Olives . . ." (Luke 22:39).

Throughout recorded scripture when the Lord needed to communicate with His children, He commanded them to be removed from the world and go into the wilderness. When prophets needed life-changing experiences or special instruction from the Lord, they went to the woods. So should we. Where should we take our young men regularly to help bring them to Christ? Young men should spend at least forty days (as Christ did) in the wilderness during their Aaronic Priesthood years, preparing for their missions. Too often we go to the outdoors only to have fun and work on merit badges. Merit badges and rank advancements earned while camping are simply the means to the end.

The following real-life stories of campouts illustrate the common lack of vision when we go into the outdoors:

A priest quorum/Venturing crew went on its traditional trip to Lake Powell, Utah, where three leaders and eight young men set up camp near the lake. One of the leaders pulled out a large cooler from the truck and announced that for the next three days the young men could have unlimited soft drinks. He was true to his word. When the cooler emptied, he drove into town and filled it with more soft drinks. For three days the priests and leaders drank soft drinks, swam and boated, and jumped off cliffs into Lake Powell. They went out to eat one night. After arriving home, one of the young men was asked by his parents if they did anything spiritual during the three days. The young man responded, "Not really. We did have prayer together at night before going to bed. But we jumped off some cool cliffs and drank lots of pop."

Another priest quorum/Venturing crew attended camp at the Teton High Adventure Camp in Wyoming. The program in camp included a raft trip down a portion of the Snake River. Under the guidance of a trained river guide from the camp staff, seven young men and two leaders began the one-day trip. One of the adult leaders jumped out of the raft after being told not to, offered boys $5 each to kiss the bus driver, and took all of the boys to town for a movie that night. He appeared to be willing to do anything to impress the young men.

In both of these examples, the adult advisers chose to go into the outdoors, then squandered the time away in worldly pursuits. Too often we go to the outdoors with nothing more than a casual, "let's have fun" attitude. The young men are better off at home than going on a casual, "let's have fun" campout. For the young men, "having fun" is usually what they anticipate in a camping experience, and the anticipation of fun and high adventure helps secure better attendance. But the adult leaders need to be thinking on a higher level.

Sometimes as leaders we try too hard to impress the young men. We mistakenly think of high adventure as something so challenging and so fun that it will tear young men away from the "high adventure" the world offers. We try to compete with the world. High adventure is an essential component of the Scouting experience. But the reason we go camping and do challenging things is to put the young men into a different world, a world more conducive to feeling the Spirit and strengthening their testimonies. Elder Harold G. Hillam tells a story that demonstrates the attitude we should have toward outdoor activities when they are done for the right reasons.

"I recall a conversation I had some years ago with my stake president in Idaho. We were discussing the forthcoming Aaronic Priesthood/ Scout campout. I explained to him that it would be necessary for each person to bring his own sleeping bag, to which the president replied, 'I have never slept in a sleeping bag.'

"I quickly responded, 'President, you can't be serious. You have lived in beautiful Idaho all these years and you have never slept in a sleeping bag?'

"'Nope!' he said, 'I never have. But I have sure lain in a lot of 'em.' And then he went on to say, 'And I'll lie in a whole bunch more of them if it will help to save boys'"(see "Sacrifice in the Service," *Ensign*, Nov. 1995, 41).

An adult leader in American Fork, Utah, remembers the effect of the outdoors on his life:

My first backpacking trip as a twelve-year-old Boy Scout left me addicted for life. It was the Thanksgiving weekend of 1984 in the mountains of Virginia. The night was clear and brisk, perfect for backpacking. We had a full moon and decided to turn off our flashlights and hike by moonlight. It was magical. The natural highs experienced while hiking and camping helped keep me away from the artificial highs of drugs and alcohol. Nature provided the needed escape every once in a while that did not harm the body, but empowered the mind and soul.

A stake president in Georgia keeps the third Friday and Saturday of each month free of stake meetings and activities and encourages all troops, teams, and crews to camp on that weekend. The stake calendar shows only Scouting campouts on the third weekend of each month. His belief: The most important metric of successful Scouting is the monthly campout, because it compels adult Scout leaders, patrol leaders' councils, and troop committees to plan and organize something. The stake president understands that each camp out should have a spiritual dimension, and encourages leaders to plan accordingly.

S. Dilworth Young, a member of the First Quorum of Seventy, said:

> Have you ever used a campfire to inspire a boy to go on a mission? . . . One of your great obligations is to teach in the environment of the outdoors that every grove can be a sacred grove, every mountaintop a Sinai. . . . You must plant in the minds of the boys as they hike and

camp, the importance of becoming a missionary" ("Scouters: Lead Them to a Mission," *Ensign,* May 1975, 98).

The method of going into the outdoors with purposeful activities planned and a spiritual antenna tuned can achieve the aims of the Boy Scouts of America and strengthen the testimonies of our young men. The monthly camping experience should be an "inspirationally induced" burst of spiritual "spring cleaning" for our young men (see Cory H. Maxwell, ed., *Neal A. Maxwell Quote Book* [Salt Lake City: Bookcraft, 1997], 325).

What do young men anticipate when going into the outdoors? They anticipate having fun, spending time with friends, eating, going fishing, hiking, and so on. What do adult advisers anticipate? I contend that if the anticipations of the youth and the adults are identical, we are not maximizing our time in the outdoors. The adult advisers should anticipate fun along with the young men, but the adults should also anticipate a spiritual dimension to the camping trip. An adviser should have a private mental list of goals for each activity regarding how he will use the opportunity to help each young man grow spiritually.

Here is a list of anticipations that captures the purpose of camping with Aaronic Priesthood young men:

THOUGHTS/ANTICIPATIONS BEFORE THE CAMPOUT

Young Men
-Canoeing
-Hiking
-Being with friends
-Making s'mores at the campfire
-Eating Brother Johnson's special
scrambled eggs

Adult Advisers
-Campfire—take the opportunity to
reflect on spiritual things
-Spend time with Cody while
hiking, get to know him better
-Talk with Sean about how the
play at school is going
-Be a canoe partner with Erik and
talk about how he is doing with
Duty to God

THOUGHTS/MEMORIES AFTER THE CAMPOUT

Young Man
-Brother Johnson is amazing;
-I felt something during the
campfire; I think it was the
beginning of a testimony

Adult Adviser
-Cody is an amazing young man
-The Spirit was strong during the
campfire; I hope Cody recognized
the Spirit

A Scoutmaster in Cedar Hills, Utah, told me that before each campout he called some of the young men's parents and asked them what he could do on the outing to help them with their son. The parents, he said, appreciated a "united front" approach to their young men.

I was fortunate to attend an LDS Scouting encampment at Camp Wisdom in Dallas, Texas. LDS Scout units from several stakes were invited for a three-day encampment led by the McKinney Texas Stake. The strategic planning for this event was evident. One of the program features on the agenda was the Book of Mormon trail.

I began walking on the trail with a dozen young men from my ward. Around the first corner we saw a campsite: Lehi and Sariah were sitting in front of a tent, and Laman and Lemuel were off to one side with hands folded, looking like they were ready to murmur. Nephi and Sam were listening intently to their parents. All the actors were in period costumes. After a short presentation, we were escorted down a hill to a meadow of blue bonnets in full bloom. We crossed the meadow to a tower where we sat and listened to King Benjamin recite powerful scripture from Mosiah 3 and 4. I was transported back in time to 124 B.C. in the land of Zarahemla. Further down the hill we listened to Alma preaching to followers by a small waterfall and lake (representing the waters of Mormon).

Next we walked up a hill and through a thick forest. There stood Helaman in full armor with some of the stripling warriors. His message was powerful and convincing. Further up the hill we encountered Captain Moroni—clad in helmet, breastplate, shield, and armor, holding aloft the title of liberty as he urged us to "come forth in the strength of the Lord, and enter into a covenant that they will maintain their rights, and their religion . . ." (Alma 46:20). I left this powerful scene thankful that I was on Captain Moroni's team—he looked like a man not to be messed with.

After a short hike, the prophet Nephi greeted us and told of his experience as he preached to the people in 23 B.C.—how he went from multitude to multitude and was rejected. He told us how he had persuaded the Lord not to destroy the people by the sword, but by a famine, that they might be humbled. The last scene on the trail was a reverent setting wherein Moroni carefully and tenderly wrapped the gold plates in a blanket and lowered them into the stone box he had prepared. Although no words were spoken, I felt the sacredness of what he held in his hands.

I have read the Book of Mormon several times, taught its truths, and felt the Spirit on many occasions while pondering its teachings, but I have never felt more connected to the book and the prophets in the book than I did that day on the Book of Mormon trail in Texas. This was truly a trail of testimony.

Scouting is simply the vehicle we use to get young men into the outdoors so they can feel the Spirit. I went to the wilderness to collect my thoughts and seek inspiration to put this manuscript together. I remember sitting on a picnic table with my laptop, smelling the nearby pine trees, watching the aspens "quake" in the soft breeze, and feeling the inspiration from above.

Adult
Association

The second "A" in PAUL SOAP is adult association.

The Scoutmaster Handbook emphasizes that boys learn a great deal by watching how adults behave, and that Scout leaders can be positive role models for the members of their troops. Those leaders who encourage and listen to the boys, demonstrating a sincere interest in them, will often have a profound influence in their lives.

Another element of adult association is the merit badge program. Have you ever thought about why we have the merit badge program? Its purpose is to introduce young men to many adults of character.

When I was a thirteen-year-old Boy Scout I wanted to earn the Athletics merit badge. My Scoutmaster signed a merit badge card giving me permission to pursue the badge. He gave me the phone number of the Athletic merit badge counselor—Dean Dixon, a member of my ward. The hardest part of the merit badge for me was gaining the courage to call Brother Dixon. With my mother's urging, I called him and set up an appointment. On the phone he suggested that I pick up the merit badge book and read the first section before we met. We then met at his home. He tested me on a few things, shared some of his knowledge, and gave me an assignment for the next meeting. We met three times and I completed the merit badge. I returned the merit badge card to the Scoutmaster. (An important note about this is that in Scouting today, no one-on-one contact is permitted. "A Scout must have a buddy with him [each time he meets] with a merit badge counselor." See *Scoutmaster Handbook*, 127.)

What happened during these three meetings with Brother Dixon? Some of his goodness and character rubbed off on me. I saw another man like my father, a man who kept his covenants and was honest and faithful. He was a second witness of what a priesthood holder should be. In its purest form, the merit badge program is simply an opportunity for a young man to associate with positive adult role models. Earning the badge is a reminder of time spent together.

Personal Growth

According to *The Scoutmaster Handbook*, boys of Scouting age are "experiencing dramatic physical and emotional growth" (p. 9). Scouting gives these boys chances to channel the energy from that growth into productive activities and to find solutions to many of their questions.

In Scouting young men should learn to enjoy serving others—to be "others focused." Young men can grow closer to Christ as they learn to serve as He did. Their testimonies can be strengthened as they see the joy of those they serve and as they themselves feel the joy of serving others. Scouts can learn and understand that "when ye are in the service of your fellow beings ye are only in the service of your God" (Mosiah 2:17).

The personal growth method also includes the Scoutmaster conference, a visit between the Scoutmaster and a Scout that is held each time the boy completes the requirements for a rank. The Scoutmaster conference is a valuable opportunity to get to know each young man, to express appreciation for him, and share your feelings about him. This conference should be a private discussion between the Scoutmaster and the Scout, but should be held in full view of other people. In addition to checking that all requirements were met, the following topics might also be appropriate for the conference:

- What he likes and dislikes about school

- Sports and hobbies he enjoys

- What he liked best about the last troop outing

- Changes he would like to see in troop meetings

- Activities he enjoys with his family

- How he defines concepts such as Scout spirit, being morally straight, and duty to God

A great way to conclude each Scoutmaster conference is to talk with the Scout about goals he would like to achieve.

VARSITY SCOUTING METHODS

Now let me introduce you to Saul Soap. Saul is a Varsity Scout, and is closely related to Paul Soap in Boy Scouting. In the LDS Church, Varsity Scouting serves boys ages fourteen and fifteen, who are also teachers in the Aaronic Priesthood. For Saul to receive the total benefits of Varsity Scouting (character, citizenship, and fitness), to draw closer to Christ, and to strengthen his testimony, he must help plan a program where each Varsity method is utilized.

Squad/Team   As in Boy Scouting, the patrol method is still the governing strategy in Varsity Scouting, except the patrol is called a squad. In Varsity Scouting, squads are in a Varsity team. While Varsity Scouting uses sports terminology, it is not a sports program.

	Boy Scouting	Varsity Scouting
Unit	Troop	Team
Small groups	Patrol	Squad
Small Group leader	Patrol Leader	Squad Leader
Adult Leader	Scoutmaster	Coach
Youth Leader	Senior Patrol Leader	Captain

Advancement   Varsity Scouts can continue their advancement through the Boy Scout ranks all the way to the Eagle Scout rank. Varsity Scouts may also be recognized for specific achievements with the Varsity Letter, Gold Letter Bar, activity pins, and the Denali Award.

Uniform   Varsity Scouts wear the same official uniform as Boy Scouts, except they wear an orange epaulette on the shirt. In addition, Varsity Scout teams are encouraged to adopt a casual uniform for activities.

Leadership   Leadership development is vital in a Varsity team. Young men ages fourteen and fifteen need hands-on opportunities to lead, and Varsity Scouting has a unique leadership structure that provides opportunities for every young man to lead.

Every Varsity Scout team should enhance its program with five fields of emphasis. Equal to one another in importance, the five are balanced in the team's program offerings and include Advancement, High Adventure/Sports, Personal

Development, Service, and Special Programs and Events.

One Varsity Scout—a program manager—is in charge of each of the five program fields of emphasis. Each program manager works closely with an adult manager to plan, organize, and lead the activities of his field of emphasis. He reports to the team captain regarding the activities, plans, and concerns. The Varsity Scout Team Organization chart below shows how the program managers fit into a large team and a small team.

Varsity Scout Team Organization

Large Team

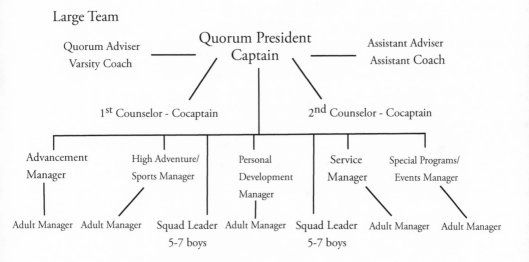

Small Team (fewer than five members)

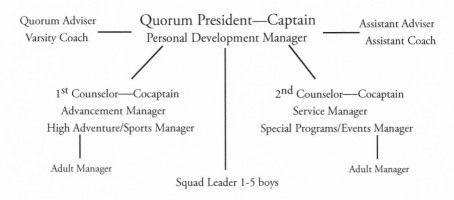

Scouting Ideals

Varsity Scouting's ideals—found in the Scout Oath, the Scout Law, the Scout Motto, and the Scout Slogan—are the same as those that every Boy Scout troop observes. Varsity Scouts have already been Boy Scouts, so they already firmly understand and believe in these ideals. To remind young men of Scouting's values, Varsity Scouting adds a Varsity Scout Pledge:

> Varsity Scout Pledge
> As a Varsity Scout I will:
> Live by the Scout Oath,
> Law, Motto, and Slogan;
> Honor the dignity and worth of all persons;
> Promote the cause of freedom; and
> Do my best to be a good team member.

Outdoors

Many Varsity Scout activities take place outdoors in settings where team members can find high adventure. It is just as important for a Varsity team to go camping monthly as it is for a Boy Scout troop.

One outdoor experience unique to Varsity Scouting is Operation On-Target. Operation On-Target is a great mountaintop experience that centers around hiking to a mountain summit and signaling to other Varsity teams located on mountain peaks within the line of sight of each other. The signaling is done with large mirrors that reflect the sun's rays into a beam of light that is visible for miles. Many Varsity teams spend weeks before the event learning specific communication skills like ham radio and signaling.

Twice in my life I have had the exhilarating mountaintop experience of seeing a beam of light pierce the haze from a mountaintop many miles away.

In California in 1986 I helped several Varsity Scout teams organize an On-Target event. Our goal was to send a beam of light from the Golden Gate Bridge in San Francisco to Mt. Rose, near Reno, Nevada. Each Varsity team adopted a peak and hiked to the top of the peak the night before. Each team had a ham radio operator with them to verify the sighting. One team was atop a building in Sacramento to help us get through the valley. On the morning of the event (usually the third Saturday of July) fog enshrouded the Golden Gate Bridge, so we drove to the top of nearby Mt. Tamalpais. I captured this event in my personal journal.

> July 19, 1986
>> I'm sitting on a park bench at the top of Mt. Tamalpais looking at a beautiful panoramic site. The fog bank is hugging the ground and the ocean. Isolated peaks and tall buildings in San Francisco pierce the dense fog like islands in a puffy sea. Twenty-three peaks will be scaled this morning, and mirrors will flash beams of light all the way to Reno. At 9:00 this morning a strong beam of light came from Mt. Diablo, forty miles away. We could hear over the radio the shouts of joy from the Scouts on Mt. Diablo as they saw our beam.

Five years later I was atop Mt. Evans near Denver, Colorado, with a Varsity team. We witnessed beams of light and heard an inspiring message from then-Elder Gordon B. Hinckley patched to us over the radio.

Many Varsity teams turn the On-Target event into a spiritual experience. After reaching the top of the mountain they bear testimonies, write down their thoughts, and put their pages into a canister that is buried in a secret place to be uncovered the next year.

Adult Association	The program manager/program adviser relationship is key to a successful Varsity team. Many crews choose a boy and his father as the manager/adviser team. Prayerful priesthood leaders will often choose a man suited to meet the spiritual needs of a young man at a very critical time of his life. Remember, no one-on-one contact is permitted.
Personal Growth	Young men of Varsity Scout age are experiencing dramatic physical and emotional growth. Personal growth can be accelerated through service projects and by inspired adult advisers.

-For further information about Varsity Scouting, contact Brad Harris at www.trailstotestimony.com

Venturing Methods

Finally, let me introduce you to Al Right, a Venturer. In the LDS Church, the sixteen- through eighteen-year-old boys are Venturers in Scouting and priests in the Aaronic Priesthood. For Al to receive the total benefits of Venturing (character, citizenship, and fitness), and to draw closer to Christ and strengthen his testimony, he must help plan a program where each Venturing method is utilized.

Adult Association	The young men lead the crew, but work in cooperation with adult leaders who serve in a "shadow" leader capacity. At this age, many young men are looking outside their home for direction in life. Adult advisers working with Priests should be more concerned with checking the spiritual pulse of each young man than with checking their handbook for signatures. Priesthood leaders can make an incredible impact on the lives of young men at this age.
Leadership	All young men are given opportunities to learn and apply proven leadership skills. Young men are taught the leadership skills of vision,

communication, listening, problem-solving, teamwork, planning, and delegation in the Venturing Leadership Skills Course (available at BSA Scout shops).

It is recommended that each Venturing crew be led by a crew president, two vice-presidents, a secretary, and a treasurer. Adult shadow leaders work with the young men to accomplish the tasks of the crew and the quorum. Activity chairs (young men) give leadership to each event, working closely with adult consultants.

Recognition

To help provide a pathway to many different experiences, the Venturing advancement program was developed; it is not really a program of advancement, but rather one of recognition. Young men can decide if they want to work on Venturing awards individually, collectively, or not at all. Don't automatically assume that your young men are excited about earning badges and awards, but young men ages sixteen to eighteen still need to be recognized with sincere compliments in front of their peers.

The Venturing awards program includes five Bronze awards, a Gold Award, a Silver Award, a Ranger Award, a Quest Award, and a T.R.U.S.T. Award. Many requirements for Venturing awards can fulfill goals and requirements of the Aaronic Priesthood Duty to God program.

Ideals

Young men are expected to know and live by the Scout Oath, Law, Motto, and Slogan. In addition, Venturing has created the Venturing Oath and Code. As Venturers, young men promise in the Venturing Oath to do their duty to God, to help strengthen America, to help others, and to seek truth and fairness.

The Venturing Code states:

> *As a Venturer, I believe that America's strength lies in our trust in God and in the courage, strength, and traditions of our people. I will, therefore, be faithful in my religious duties and will maintain a personal sense of honor in my own life. I will treasure my American heritage and will do all I can to preserve and enrich it. I will recognize the dignity and worth of all humanity and will use fair play and goodwill in my daily life.; I will acquire the Venturing attitude that seeks truth in all things and adventure on the frontiers of our changing world.*

Group Activities

Venturing doesn't promote patrols. However, the crew can be organized to best meet the needs of the young men. Learning by doing in a group setting provides opportunities for developing new skills.

High Adventure

The Venturing emphasis on high adventure helps provide team-building in an outdoor setting; the lifelong memories that are created will help keep young men close to their quorum members, advisers, and priesthood leaders. Each high adventure activity should be planned by the young men and should have strategically planned spiritual moments.

Teaching Others

This is a unique feature of Venturing. All the Venturing awards require young men to teach what they have learned to others. When they teach, they are better able to retain the skill or knowledge and gain confidence in their ability to speak and relate to others. This feature provides hands-on training for teaching in the mission field.

When leaders of sixteen- to eighteen-year-old young men think of "Venturing," some may mistakenly correlate it with "Scouts" (with the associated merit badges, knots, basic first aid, uniforms, and so on). Unfortunately, they then dismiss this exciting program as not being in tune with the needs or interests of these older boys.

Many priests quorums struggle with quality Young Men activity nights. Those who have attained Eagle rank may feel that activity night is no longer important because they are no longer pursuing Scouting ranks. Many priest-age young men tell their parents and priesthood leaders that they are not interested in Scouting—because their view of "Scouting" includes nothing more than earning merit badges, wearing the uniform, and enduring pressure from parents to earn their Eagle. These perceptions are very real and often negatively affect the success of priest quorum activities.

Venturing is a totally different activity program, tailored exactly to the needs and interests of high-school-aged young men to prepare them for missions and adult life. Venturing is a set of focused resources that are wholesome, flexible, and challenging for sixteen- to eighteen-year-old young men while achieving the purposes of the Aaronic Priesthood.

Every priest quorum is unique—and Venturing is flexible enough to be tailored to each quorum's needs. Each crew is expected to have youth leaders; they can be the same as the quorum leaders, or can be different young men. The actual positions can be changed or combined to meet the individual needs of the quorum.

The young men in the quorum/crew decide if they want to wear a uniform. Venturing does not have a *required* uniform. The recommended uniform is a spruce-green shirt with charcoal gray pants, but the uniform, if any, is the choice of the crew. Many crews choose a polo shirt of their own design.

In October 2006 an LDS Venturing Usage Survey was conducted by the Boy Scouts of America National Office Research Service. The Venturing Division of the Boy Scouts of America was interested in learning more about how wards of The Church of Jesus Christ of Latter-day Saints in the United States use the Venturing program and program tools in their ministry.

Questionnaires were mailed to 2,941 LDS Bishops randomly selected from the database in the BSA National office. To verify wards that had registered Venturing crews and those that did not, the mailing list was cross-referenced with the BSA registration database. Surveys were color-coded; 1,474 wards with registered Venturing crews received a survey printed on buff-colored paper, and 1,467 wards that did not have a registered crew (yes, that many wards without a crew!) received a survey printed on white paper. Both surveys contained identical questions. A total of 522 completed surveys were collected.

The survey revealed that nine years after Venturing was created, many wards were still unaware of the program and many had not implemented the program.

- 19 percent of bishops surveyed didn't know if their ward had a Venturing crew.

- Only 47.6 percent of wards with Venturing crews know about the Venturing Leadership Skills Course.

- Only 9.4 percent of youth leaders in Venturing crews had completed the Venturing Leadership Skills Course.

- Fewer than 1 percent of Venturers had earned Venturing awards.

The survey also revealed the benefits to the wards that had successfully implemented Venturing:

- Wards with Venturing crews had larger priests quorums—10.2 young men—than wards with no Venturing crews—7.7 young men.

- Wards with Venturing crews had a higher percentage of ordained priests—72.5 percent to 57.1 percent.

- Wards with Venturing crews had a higher percentage of Eagle Scouts—28.4 percent to 16.8 percent.

- Wards with Venturing crews had a higher percentage of young men working on the Duty to God program—49.0 percent to 41.6 percent.

- Wards with Venturing crews were more likely to have an annual calendar—78.9 percent to 59.0 percent.

- Wards with Venturing crews were more likely to have priest assistants conduct presidency meetings—35.8 percent to 18.7 percent.

Priests quorums that were also Venturing crews out-performed in every measurable category the priests quorums that were not Venturing crews.

A Venturing leader called me and told me that he was a complete failure as a leader because none of his priests were interested in earning Venturing awards. I assured him that earning awards in Venturing is a measurement of activity and success, but not the only measure.

A stake Young Men's president in Provo, Utah, visited each of the priest quorums in his stake and discovered that all were registered Venturing crews, but none of them were "doing" Venturing. He determined that the ward Aaronic Priesthood advisers in his stake hadn't seen a model of a successful Venturing crew, so he decided to create one. One evening each month his stake provided a Venturing activity for all bishops, priest quorum/crew advisers, and priests in the stake. The stake conducted an activity interest survey with the young men and determined outdoor activities they would like to do, and conducted the Program Capability Inventory to determine resources available. One month the stake conducted the Venturing Leadership Skills Course, modeling to the ward leaders how to do it. For the next several months the stake assigned each ward to conduct an activity. More than 80 percent of the priests in the stake attended these monthly Venturing activities and adult advisers and youth leaders learned how to do Venturing by seeing and doing.

DEFINING SUCCESS IN A PRIESTS QUORUM/VENTURING CREW
1. Young men have completed the activity interest survey.

2. Adults in the ward have completed the Program Capability Inventory.

    (The surveys listed above can be obtained by going to google.com/ LDS Venturing Guide)

3. The quorum/crew has a "draft" annual calendar and a working three-month calendar that includes activities chosen by the young men and that utilizes consultants from the ward.

4. Mutual is led by youth activity chairs.

5. Young men have opportunities to teach others.

6. The Venturing Leadership Skills Course has been conducted by the youth.

7. The quorum/crew presidency has defined duties and meets as needed to plan and administer the program. Boys lead with adult shadow leaders.

My experience has shown that if a priests quorum/Venturing crew accomplishes these seven items, they can expect to have increased attendance at mutual and quorum meetings. Quorum unity will improve, and the young men will feel empowered and will take more ownership in the quorum/crew.

If these conditions are in place, more young men to will be worthy to receive the Melchezidek Priesthood, receive temple endowments, and serve honorable full-time missions. In other words, when properly implemented, Venturing is a missionary preparation program for priests in the Aaronic Priesthood.

For more information about Venturing contact Brad Harris at www. trailstotestimony.com

Chapter 9: Conducting Reflections

One of the best ways to apply gospel principles in the laboratory of the outdoors is by conducting reflections. While I was serving as a Venturing crew adviser in Utah, my crew went canoeing on Utah Lake. It was very windy out on the lake. High waves made canoeing very difficult, and many of the youth were losing the battle against the wind. In spite of their efforts, their canoes were drifting away from the harbor. I sent some of the stronger canoeists out to rescue the weaker ones. I was in the back of my canoe, stroking as hard as I could, trying to keep the front of the canoe perpendicular to the waves and directly into the wind. I focused on a tree near our destination and pointed the bow of the canoe toward the tree. I noticed that if I made each stroke strong and hard, I was able to make progress. If my strokes were weak or the technique was faulty, I made little progress. Eventually all the canoes arrived safely inside the protection of the harbor, where the wind and waves were hindered by a rock jetty. The crew gratefully pulled the canoes out of the water and on to the shore.

We stood on the shore, wearing our life jackets and holding our paddles. At this point I conducted a reflection—simply stated, encouraging the youth to talk about their experiences immediately after they happen. Experiences are more meaningful and effective if reflected on.

Reflection provides an opportunity to ponder the spiritual applications of temporal experience. Each member of the group should share their thoughts. As leaders, we need to actively plan times during which *everyone* gets a chance for input, or else those individuals who are less assertive or confident might never say anything, even if they have valuable insights.

There are four simple ground rules of reflection. First, no putdowns are allowed; every response is welcome and valid. Second, the person conducting the session should not show disapproval of a response or a person, either verbally or nonverbally.

Reflection is best accomplished by asking open-ended questions such as, "What?," "How?," "When?," and "Where?" In reflection, there is no right or wrong answers. Ask positive questions first, such as, "What was good about the way decisions were made?" or "What did the group do well?" Then you can ask about improvement: "What was the problem with the way you were communicating?" or "Were there any problems with what happened?" This is the evaluation part of reflection. And finally, conduct the reflection immediately after the event, so that memories of the experience are fresh. Don't wait until next Sunday to reflect on weeknight or Saturday activities.

Conclude the reflection by striving to recognize a spiritual application. At Utah Lake after the canoeing activity I asked, "What did we learn today from this activity? What were some of the problems we encountered? How did we overcome them?" I told the group how I focused on the tree on the shore to help guide me safely to the shore. Then I asked, "How could we make this a spiritual application? What might the tree represent?"

One of the Venturers said, "The tree could be the priesthood, or Jesus Christ." "That's good," I said. "What about the wind and the waves?"

Another Venturer said, "They could be the temptations of Satan or trials in our lives." I responded, "Just like I focused on the tree to help me through the wind and waves, if we focus on Christ we can overcome the temptations of Satan and be guided through our trials. I also noticed that when I used the proper technique with my paddle and concentrated on strong strokes, the canoe moved faster and led me through the wind and waves better. The proper technique and strong strokes could be like daily scripture study and prayer; they help us overcome temptations and progress spiritually."

As the Venturers left for home after this canoeing event, they weren't thinking, "Wow, that was fun!" Instead, they were thinking about the importance of focusing on Jesus Christ to help them overcome the temptations of Satan, and on the importance of daily personal prayer and scripture study to help them progress spiritually. Canoeing was simply the catalyst that provided an environment where young men could talk about spiritual things.

This is why we go canoeing. This is why we go rock climbing or hiking—to provide an opportunity to conduct a spiritual reflection. Most Scout activities should end with a reflection, and young men should leave these activities thinking about the spiritual application at the end of the activity.

After modeling how to do a reflection several times, your spiritual antenna will be finely tuned. Once you've shown them how it's done, allow young men to lead reflections. At the beginning of an event ask a young man to be prepared to conduct a reflection after the activity. He will work at tuning his spiritual antenna throughout the event. You will be surprised how well the young men do at conducting reflections and responding to open-ended questions.

At Camp Bradley in Idaho (by the way, Camp Bradley is one of the finest of the forty Scout camps I have visited) I gave a presentation to LDS Scout leaders about conducting reflections. After the presentation one of the men approached me. He told me he had never heard of the concept of reflection before. He said, "The entire week at camp has been focused solely on earning merit badges. Our troop is leaving camp tomorrow; what can I do to salvage our week?"

I suggested he get the boys together in an unhurried atmosphere before they leave for home and ask open-ended questions about what they learned in camp: What are you grateful for? What has happened at camp that will help you be a better person when you get home? I suggested he try to generate a spiritual tone by sharing his thoughts about each of the young men. He could think of instances during the week where boys helped others, learned new skills, or gained a new appreciation for something. I suggested he mention some of those experiences to draw the young men into the conversation.

A stake Young Men's president in Texas said the following at a Little Philmont training in 2004:

> Last year another leader and I took six youth on a three-day backpacking trip. For some this was their first wilderness experience. We hiked about twenty-five miles, soaked in a 100-degree hot springs of crystal clear water one night, and crossed the Gila River about forty times. We experienced physical pain, hunger, thirst, and fatigue under priesthood supervision. Several times during the hike we stopped and reflected.
>
> One of the reflections happened as we crossed the river the first time. As we walked on the stones to cross the river, some stones looked

trustworthy, but they turned if you stepped on them. Others were firm. At one point I told the boys that people are like stones: some you can trust and some you cannot. I suggested that they choose their friends wisely.

Each night we read from the Book of Mormon together before going to bed. On the last day after we hiked out of a deep canyon, we had a testimony meeting. These young men bore strong testimonies of the Savior and His power.

When one of the young men got home, his mother told him that while he was backpacking, his father had moved out and had filed for divorce. This deacon told his mother, "If I can get off the mountain, I can overcome this too."

The next day was fast and testimony meeting. Each of the youth bore testimonies. Their conclusions about the three-day hike included observations that when we read the scriptures together in the wilderness, we were nourished; we learned things in the wilderness that we couldn't learn anywhere else.

A Stake Young Men's president in Arizona related the following to me in 2010:

This past weekend we had a district camporee and this particular ward attended with all their age groups (Webelos through Venturing). On Saturday we had roughly 15 stations/events that the groups could rotate through. Events ranged from Ethical Debate, to Archery, Stretcher Relays, BB/Rifle Ranges, and Rappelling. The unit leaders conducted a reflection at the conclusion of each event. The results were incredible.

Yesterday, several young men and several of the adult leaders bore their testimonies in their Fast Sunday Sacrament Meeting about their Scouting experience that weekend and how it impacted them spiritually. It was a very powerful testament to the purpose of the scouting program and the simple technique of reflections.

A BYU student told a poignant story in responding to a final exam essay question. The question on the exam was: "You've been hiking all day with eight fourteen- and fifteen-year-olds and one other leader. You've climbed several thousand feet and you're sitting at the top of a tall peak. The group has encountered rocks and boulders, heat, discomfort from the packs, blisters on their feet, etc. Conduct a reflection from the mountaintop. What would you say?"

The student answered: "This situation actually happened to me, except that I was one of the boys. If I were the leader, I would do what my bishop did. I would gather everyone together for a brief word of prayer. I would have the boys look around and point out that what they were seeing is reverent to our Heavenly Father. It is a testimony that God lives. The view from the mountaintop is better than any other view. Such are the stages of life. At times we reach a 'peak' in life and feel that we can see clearly both in front and behind us. Then there are times where life is spent climbing up a peak. Those times are hard. We need to remember the times that we have been on a peak when we are in the valleys, so that we can get through those hard times. I would tell the boys never to forget that view. I still have not forgotten it many years later."

Conducting a reflection helps remind young men that "there is a God" and that all things bear record of Him (Alma 30:44). A reflection provides a fertile environment for a young man to "treasure up . . . the words of life" (D&C 84:85). Small group settings in the outdoors are the most conducive to spiritual sharing. Working, playing, praying, and being together provides adults and young men opportunities to learn and grow, and Scouting activities provide the natural setting for this kind of interaction.

In my ward, we taught the young women adults and youth to conduct reflections. Now at each combined activity each month, the group or quorum in charge, concludes the event with a group reflection.

Chapter 10: When Properly Carried Out

The LDS *Scouting Handbook* states that when properly carried out, under the direction of priesthood leaders, Scouting not only supplements the activities of Aaronic Priesthood quorums, but helps accomplish the eternal purposes of the priesthood and families.

"When properly carried out" means that the adult leaders know and understand the aims, and implement the methods, of the Boy Scouts of America. When Scouting is properly carried out, there are at least seven major benefits to young men, adults, families, and the Church:

1. Scouting teaches values that are in harmony with gospel principles.
2. Scouting can provide opportunities to practice and apply gospel principles in the laboratory of the outdoors.
3. Scouting promotes family unity.
4. Scouting can be a tool to strengthen the quorum.
5. Scouting can be a powerful missionary tool.
6. Scouting prepares young men for full-time missionary service.
7. Scouting can accelerate a young man's spiritual progression.

WHEN PROPERLY CARRIED OUT, SCOUTING TEACHES VALUES THAT ARE IN HARMONY WITH GOSPEL PRINCIPLES.

Looking carefully for similarities and differences, I compared the literature prepared by the Church for the youth with the literature published by the Boy Scouts of America. In the statements below, you be the judge. Are the statements to the youth from the Church and the Boy Scouts in harmony? Read the two statements on each of these seven subjects, then try to determine which one comes from an LDS Church publication and which comes from a Boy Scouts of America publication. (The answers are found in the appendix.)

1—Statements on Drugs

A. Some drugs are prescribed by doctors to ease pain or relieve symptoms of disease, but prescription drugs are dangerous if they are misused. You should never take a prescription drug unless it is prescribed for you by a doctor. All other drugs are dangerous for you—whether they have been legally prescribed for someone else or sold illegally on the street.

B. Any drug, chemical, or dangerous practice that is used to produce a sensation or "high" can destroy physical, mental, and spiritual well-being. These include hard drugs, prescription or over-the-counter medications that are abused, and household chemicals.

2—Statements on Alcohol

A. The use of alcoholic beverages is prohibited. Serious consequences can result from the use of alcoholic beverages.

B. Any form of alcohol is harmful to your body and spirit. . . . Drinking can lead to alcoholism, which destroys individuals and families.

3—Statements on Tobacco

A. Never use tobacco products, such as cigarettes, snuff, chewing tobacco, cigars, and pipe tobacco. They are very addictive and will damage your body and shorten your life.

B. Don't be fooled. Smoking shortens your breath. . . . Smoke coats your lungs with sticky tars that have been shown to cause cancer and emphysema, diseases that kill hundreds of thousands of people every year.

4—Statements on Other Harmful Substances

A. Do not drink coffee or tea, for these are addictive and harmful.

B. Coffee, tea, and many cola drinks contain *caffeine,* a mild stimulant that temporarily stirs up the nervous system and speeds the heart. Caffeine can make you irritable and cause you to have difficulty sleeping.

5—Statements on Sexual Purity

A. Sex should take place only between people who are married to each other.

B. God has commanded that sexual intimacy be reserved for marriage.

6—Statements on Choosing Friends

A. Choose friends who share your values so you can strengthen and encourage each other in living high standards

B. Choose friends whose values you admire, but don't turn down the chance to get to know someone because he or she is not just like the rest of your friends.

7—Statements on Language

A. Swear words and dirty stories are often used as weapons to ridicule other people and hurt their feelings. The same is true of racial slurs and jokes that make fun of ethnic groups or people with physical or mental limitations. . . . there is no kindness or honor in such tasteless behavior.

B. Foul language harms your spirit and degrades you. Do not let others influence you to use it. Choose friends who use good language. Help others around you use clean language by your example and by good-naturedly encouraging them to choose other words.

Can you see from this exercise why the Church adopts Scouting? The values taught by Scouting ratify the values taught by the Church. Parents and priesthood leaders should have complete confidence that Scouting teaches values in harmony with gospel principles.

WHEN PROPERLY CARRIED OUT, SCOUTING CAN PROVIDE OPPORTUNITIES TO PRACTICE AND APPLY GOSPEL PRINCIPLES IN THE LABORATORY OF THE OUTDOORS. "Scouting should help young men put into practice the gospel principles they learn on Sunday." (*Administering the Church, book 2, 2010*, pg. 59)

Have you considered occasionally connecting a Scouting activity or even a campout to a Sunday lesson? Here are some examples:

- On Sunday in the deacons quorum we taught Lesson # 49, "Using Time Wisely." On Wednesday night the young men completed requirements #8a–d of the Personal Management merit badge. A reflection was conducted at the conclusion of the meeting, tying the Sunday lesson with the activity on Wednesday. Boy Scouting can be the laboratory for applying gospel principles taught on Sunday.

- On Sunday in the teachers quorum we taught Lesson #6, "Christlike Service." On Wednesday the Varsity Scouts conducted a service project for an elderly widow in the ward, and the service hours counted towards their Star and Life ranks. A reflection was conducted at the conclusion of the meeting, connecting the Sunday lesson with the service rendered on Wednesday. Varsity Scouting can be the laboratory for practicing what was taught on Sunday.

- On Sunday in the priests quorum, we taught Lesson #39, "Feasting on the Words of Christ," about the importance of daily scripture reading. At a campout the next Friday night, the young men read selected scriptures around the campfire with their adviser, a reflection was conducted, then each boy voluntarily bore his testimony of scripture study. Venturing can be the laboratory to help young men apply what they learned in the quorum meeting on Sunday.

No campout should be conducted just for the sake of camping. Each outdoor experience should be carefully crafted to create an ideal setting where the young men can feel the Spirit and feel closer to their Heavenly Father. A Venturing crew adviser in Arizona was surprised when his bishop suggested they fast on the Thursday before a scheduled weekend camping experience to help them create spiritual moments for the young men. This adviser reported that his spiritual preparation was rewarded with a very meaningful, Spirit-filled camping experience.

An experienced Scouter in El Paso, Texas, who has led hundreds of boys on fifty-milers said, "I never take youth into the back country to go camping. I take them to be with their Maker. Do we go to less active boys and say, 'Put on your tie and come to Church for three hours?' No—I say, 'Come with us on this fifty-miler.'"

WHEN PROPERLY CARRIED OUT, SCOUTING PROMOTES FAMILY UNITY.
> Akela is a good leader.
> Your mother or father or other adult member of your family is Akela.
> In the pack, your Cubmaster is Akela.
> Your den leader is Akela.
> At school, your teacher is Akela (*Cub Scout Wolf Handbook* [TX: Boy Scouts of America, 2005], 20).

At the bottom of every page in the Wolf and Bear book is a line that says, "Akela's OK," with a place for Akela to sign. The Cub Scout program, if carried out properly, is designed to have the Cub Scout's parent sign as Akela most of the time. Most of the requirements in the Wolf and Bear books are best accomplished at home.

Cub Scouting is hundreds of father-son and mother-son outings waiting to happen, not just a checklist to complete so a boy can receive the award.

The Family: A Proclamation to the World reminds us that successful marriages and families are established and maintained on a number of things, including "wholesome recreational activities." What is wholesome recreation? Can Scouting assist families in fulfilling this charge?

Many Boy Scout councils offer family camping facilities. The Trapper Trails Council in Ogden, Utah, and the Utah National Parks council in Provo, Utah have recently created family camps. Camp Bartlett and Camp TIFIE provide age-appropriate activities for families and spouses while leaders are trained. Instead of leaving their families for a week in order to be trained, Scout leaders bring their families along. For example, while one father attended Woodbadge, his fourteen-year-old son went to National Youth Leadership Training, and his wife and other children participated in family camp. On Monday night, everyone came together for an opening campfire.

The Philmont Training Center (PTC) in New Mexico provides a unique environment for the training of volunteer and professional leaders. Each summer, more than 6,000 Scouters and family members attend PTC, which offers a full, organized program for every member of the family—from infants to spouses. Family members are joined by others in their age group and participate in a carefully designed, age- and ability-specific program under the leadership of trained, experienced staff. Activities include hiking, tours, handicrafts, games, campfires, and outdoor activities.

Philmont is also the site of the Priesthood Leadership Conference under the direction of the Young Men General Presidency and the General Scouting Committee of the Church. The faculty, selected from the Young Men General Board and Primary General Presidency and General Board, provides training in the program and administration of Scouting as a supporting activity of the Aaronic Priesthood and Primary. An invitation from the First Presidency to attend as well as information concerning the Philmont Leadership Conference is sent to every stake president in the United States and Canada each November. The LDS Scouting Leadership

Conference at Philmont is for Stake Presidency members and their families. Due to the high demand to attend the conference, only stake presidency members will be immediately registered. In addition, if members of the stake presidency register and would like a high councilor and/or stake Young Men president to attend with them, those applications will be immediately accepted as long as space is available. All other applications will be placed on a waiting list. The training conference is actually a family vacation; while the priesthood leaders attend conference sessions, wives and children participate in programs that include tours, crafts, hikes, or just relaxing. Full-day activities with leaders are provided for each group.

WHEN PROPERLY CARRIED OUT, SCOUTING CAN BE A TOOL TO STRENGTHEN THE QUORUM.

Using Scouting properly can greatly assist Aaronic Priesthood quorums reach out to less-active members. The "sizzle" of fun Scouting activities attracts young men better than the prospect of putting on a tie and sitting through three hours of church on Sunday. Invitations to participate in Scouting activities extended to less-active boys by active young men and adult advisers to less active boys should be standard operating procedure in a quorum.

A priesthood quorum is (Stephen L. Richards, "A Priesthood Quorum: Three-fold Definition," *Conference Report,* April 7, 1939):

1.	A Class:	A place where a young man may be taught the gospel of Jesus Christ, how to live its teachings, and feel the Holy Spirit.
2.	A Brotherhood:	To strengthen, build, lift, and friendship each other.
3.	A Service Unit:	To provide opportunities for service to quorum members and others.

President Hinckley asked us as members to provide for every member of the Church "a friend, a responsibility, and nurturing with the good word of God" (Gordon B. Hinckley, *Conference Report,* April 1997, 47).

A priesthood quorum can help us meet President Hinckley's challenge. Sunday lessons (the class) in the quorum provides nurturing by the good word of God. The brotherhood in the quorum provides friends for young men. The service unit provides opportunities to accept responsibility.

A priests quorum/crew adviser told me this story about one of his young men: eighteen and no longer participating in Scouting activities, Robert was starting to drift away; he attended only occasionally on Sunday. He told his leaders that he didn't like Scouting, had no plans of going on a mission, and was going to enlist in the military after graduating high school. Robert's crew adviser talked him into attending a whitewater rafting trip with the other priests. He loved the activity. His attendance on Sunday and at activities increased. Robert became active in the priests quorum and when the time came, submitted his mission papers. His mother was astonished at the change that came over her son. She asked the adviser, "What did you do on that campout? My son is a different kid!"

A brother from Hawaii related the following story about how Scouting can help build the quorum:

> As Scoutmasters we are always looking for ways to introduce more boys to the ideals of Scouting and, along the way, to fellowship them into the gospel. That opportunity presented itself one Sunday. A family of three boys (ages nine, ten, and twelve) that had been less active in the Church arrived for sacrament meeting. They were a wonderful family, but just weren't committed to participating in the Church or Boy Scouting. Apparently the gospel in Hawaii was less appealing than other activities and distractions at the same time.
>
> Immediately following sacrament services I approached James, the twelve-year-old, reached out to shake his hand, and at the same time extended an invitation for him to join us on our Scouting overnighter that Friday at Bellows Beach. His eyes gleamed with excitement and anticipation and he eagerly accepted that one simple invitation, which quickly lead from one thing to another. Soon he became active in Scouting and was our best senior patrol leader—not to mention our best banana pancake chef.
>
> Because of his involvement in Scouting and the quality fellowshipping from his quorum, the family eventually became active in the Church. His father was called to be the bishop of our ward, his two younger brothers

became Eagle Scouts, all three served honorable full-time missions, and James was sealed to his eternal companion in the Laie Temple.

Each young man should be visited in his home by his quorum presidency at each stage of his advancement in the priesthood. A deacons quorum in Utah sends the presidency, three in white shirts and ties and one in a Scouting uniform, to show a new young man and his parents the proper dress for Sunday meeting and Scouting activities. The presidency delivers the *For the Strength of Youth* pamphlet, the Duty to God booklet, and a three-month calendar of Scouting activities.

The Aaronic Priesthood quorum and Scouting serve as a shepherd for all the members of the quorum. The prophet Ezekiel helps define the role of a shepherd: "For thus saith the Lord God; Behold, I, even I, will both search my sheep, and seek them out. As a shepherd seeketh out his flock in the day that he is among his sheep that are scattered; so will I seek out my sheep, and will deliver them out of all places where they have been scattered in the cloudy and dark day" (Ezek. 34:11–12).

WHEN PROPERLY CARRIED OUT, SCOUTING CAN BE A POWERFUL MISSIONARY TOOL. Scouting can provide an excellent opportunity to share the gospel of Jesus Christ with others. Because of the appeal of the outdoors for young men, many rich opportunities are made available for planting gospel seeds. I have heard dozens of stories of adult Scouters who claim that Scouting was the principle reason they belong to the Church. I share with you a few of these conversion stories.

A BYU student named Pat shared the following story with me:

> I grew up in Mobile, Alabama. I was raised in the Methodist church and joined a Boy Scout troop at church. I was active in my church until I went away to college, where I fell away from my church habits and developed some bad ones instead, mostly drinking alcohol. I didn't do well in college and decided to work at Philmont Scout Ranch in New Mexico. Philmont changed my life. It helped me find a purpose in my life. The director of the training center at Philmont was a Mormon, and we had several discussions about religion. He knew the Old and New Testament bet-

ter than I did. During the summer of 2001 I went to the LDS chapel at Philmont with some LDS friends; it was fast and testimony meeting, and I was touched.

That fall the year-round staff at Philmont went on a recruiting trip to BYU. For thirteen hours in the car the six of us—three Methodists, one Catholic, a Buddhist, and a Mormon—talked about religion. While in Utah I saw the movie *The Testaments* and took a tour of Temple Square. Back in Philmont I asked my boss for a copy of the Book of Mormon.

That book unlocked a door in my soul. After sacrament meeting a few weeks later I met two guys named "Elder," and they asked me if I would like to take the discussions. I was baptized in April 2003. While at Philmont I met my future wife. We were sealed in the Boise Temple on May 15, 2004.

A BYU student named Adam shared with me his conversion story:

> I grew up in Littleton, Colorado. There was no strong religious tradition in my family; I grew up with no spiritual inclinations and no affiliation with a church. One day a new family moved into my neighborhood. They had boys my age, and we became fast friends. My friends invited me to attend their Scouting meetings and campouts. I discovered that they were Mormons and was a little taken back at first, but it felt good to be with them. On Scouting campouts I was introduced to prayer. I felt the Spirit the most through service projects, and that had a huge impact on my life. Through those experiences, I became a "service addict."
>
> When I saw my LDS friends gaining testimonies of their own, I felt a deficit in my life. Once I felt comfortable in the church building on mutual nights, I then accepted the invitation to attend seminary. I received a triple combination from the seminary teacher and read the Book of Mormon. It felt good to read this book and it seemed good and true.

As I was reading section 9 of the Doctrine and Covenants, I related to Oliver Cowdery, who was challenged to "study it out in your mind; then you must ask me if it be right." I experienced the same feeling while reading the scriptures that I felt while doing service projects, and realized that the feeling came from the Spirit.

One evening while I was pondering the scriptures in my room I felt driven to my knees. I prayed with real intent, felt the Spirit, and knew that the Church was true. I promised Heavenly Father I would tell other people about the gospel and serve the best I could.

I started regularly attending church on Sundays and took the missionary discussions at a friend's home. I felt the same confirming witness from the Spirit each time I met with the missionaries.

I was baptized at age seventeen, served a mission in Germany, and married in the temple. Scouting began my journey to finding the truth by introducing me to the Spirit through service and prayer.

In the summer of 1985 I was the camp director at Camp Wolfeboro, located in the High Sierras of California. I lived in a cabin in the camp with my wife and three children for three months. Staff members were often visiting us in our cabin in the evening when it was time to have family scripture study and family prayer. We always invited them to join us in our nightly tradition. One staff member, Dane, showed an unusual interest in being with our family. During the summer he learned to pray vocally for the first time and he read the Book of Mormon with us.

After camp we invited Dane to take the missionary discussions in our home. The full-time missionaries taught him, and he was baptized. Dane was later married and sealed in the Oakland Temple.

An LDS den leader in Arizona witnessed the missionary power of Cub Scouting. A non-member Cub Scout in her den observed the other boys praying each week. One week he asked the den leader if he could give the closing prayer in the den meeting. A touching moment occurred as she helped the young Cub Scout pray vocally for the first time. Later, the young man expressed the desire to pursue the Faith in God award along with his fellow Cub Scouts.

A Scoutmaster in Florida (who I met at Philmont) shared how the Scouting program in his ward became an integral part of the ward mission:

> In 2006 I was called to be a Scoutmaster in a branch in Florida. Only one young man was in the branch. I read the scriptures and prayed for guidance and began to invite boys from the neighborhood to join our troop. Soon, other young men were participating in weekly Scouting activities. Many of the new Scouts enjoyed the fellowship of the LDS-sponsored troop so much that they began attending on Sunday. Baptisms soon followed. In five years, the branch grew from one young man to 28. The branch grew from 24 members to 120 members in the same time period. One of our young men has just returned from his mission, and is attending BYU. We expect many more missionaries.

WHEN PROPERLY CARRIED OUT, SCOUTING PREPARES YOUNG MEN FOR FULL-TIME MISSIONARY SERVICE.

President Thomas S. Monson recently admonished the young men of the Church; "..to the young men of the Aaronic Priesthood...I repeat what prophets have long taught – that every worthy, able young man should prepare to serve a mission...prepare for service as a missionary." (Thomas S. Monson, "As We Meet Together Again", *Ensign,*, November 2010, pgs. 5-6)

And from President Ezra Taft Benson, "Give me a young man who has kept himself morally clean and has faithfully attended his Church meetings. Give me a young man who has magnified his priesthood and has earned the Duty to God Award and is an Eagle Scout. Give me a young man who is a seminary graduate and has a burning testimony of the Book of Mormon. Give me such a young man, and I will give you a young man who can perform miracles for the Lord in the mission field and throughout his life" ("To the 'Youth of the Noble Birthright,'" *Ensign,* May 1986, 45).

Administering the Church states, "The earlier a young man decides to serve a mission, the more likely it is that he will serve." (Book 2, 55) I visited a stake in Utah that conducted a missionary fireside for all the eleven year old boys in the stake and their parents. At the fireside each boy was encouraged to make a public commitment to serve a mission. Each boy signed a certificate along with the Stake President, Bishop and parents. The certificate stated they were going to serve a mission. Each young man received a bronze coin. On one side of the coin was engraved the picture of John the Baptist ordaining Joseph Smith and Oliver Cowdery to the Aaronic Priesthood. On the other side of the coin was engraved, "Missionary class of 2017" (the year these young men turned 19).

Can Scouting prepare young men ages 8 - 18 for full-time missionary service? Is it possible that a properly applied Scouting program can help young men prepare for missions? Is there a connection between successful missionary service and a dynamic Aaronic Priesthood/Scouting program? A study was conducted at Brigham Young University in which recently returned missionaries were asked if involvement in the Aaronic Priesthood/ Scouting program helped them as missionaries. Just look at the summaries of a few of those interviews:

An elder who served in Illinois:

- Without Scouting my mission would have been much more difficult.

- As a Scout I was taught to set an example to others. As a missionary I was expected to be a constant example.

- I can't think of anything that better prepared me for a mission than Scouting did.

An elder who served in Mexico:

- I learned as a Scout to get along with others and other basic people skills.

- This foundation helped me on my mission to adjust to new companions and effectively work with people.

- Scouting taught me how to survive and to stand on my own two feet. This was daily practice in Mexico.

An elder who served in England:

- When I was district leader I often had flashbacks when I was Senior Patrol Leader. I used the same skills.

- As a Scout I was taught one night how to patch a hole in sheet rock. I had an opportunity to apply that skill in England.

- In Scouts we went biking all the time and learned to repair them. In the mission field we were constantly fixing our bikes.

- I can't imagine what I would have done with my time that would have better prepared me for my mission and my life.

An elder who served in Washington state:

- It dawned on me that "Be Prepared" should be my motto as a missionary just as it was in Scouting. I was always asked to do something that required preparation.

- As a leader in the mission, when I encountered difficult situations from other Elders, I was able to handle them because I had been down this road before as a leader in Scouting.

An elder who served in Honduras:

- Scouting taught me the value of completing goals and to finish what I started. This was valuable training for my mission.

- I learned basic first aid skills in Scouting which were applied several times in Honduras.

- As a Scout I learned to budget money (Personal Management merit badge). In the mission field I was given a set amount of money each month and had to manage it.

- I was taught outdoor skills like the importance of hydration, wearing appropriate shoes and socks, poisonous plants, all of which I applied walking through the jungles of Honduras.

- Scouting introduced me to the culture of uniform as an equalizer. As a missionary I wore a uniform

An elder who served in the Philippines:

- We had to lash bamboo furniture to sit on in our apartment.

- Water purification that I learned on backpacking trips I used in the mission.

- Scouting taught me not to micromanage (Eagle Service Project). I used this skill as a Zone Leader.

- As a Scout I learned to sew on patches, in the Philippines I often had to sew on buttons.

- First Aid merit badge taught me to treat blisters and cuts. We encountered these situations often in the mission field.

- We built an elevated sidewalk (using lashings) for a mother to have safe passage from her home over raw sewage.

An elder who served in the Brazil:

- The use of compass skills I learned as a Scout helped me navigate the jungles and cities of Brazil.

- The concept of self-motivation I learned in Scouting helped me succeed in serving and teaching without having a task master.

An elder who served in Japan:

- My Swiss army knife was the most useful non-spiritual tool used on my mission. I repaired bicycles, did first aid, etc.

- I built snow caves as a Scout in Oregon. In Japan we often had to dig through snow to get out of our apartment.

- The concept of layering my clothing was used in -40 weather in Japan.

- Map and compass skills were used daily to get around.

- In the mission field I applied leadership skills I learned as a Scout.

- The food I ate on campouts prepared me for whatever the Japanese fed me.

- Being more prepared for life in general and more confident in my abilities to care for myself freed me to focus on matters more spiritual.

An elder who served in the Portugal:

- Scouting taught me respect for peer leaders. On my mission I had peer leaders, and I learned to receive counsel without taking offense.

- The Eagle project taught me that I could do something that first seemed impossible. At first Portuguese seemed impossible.

An elder who served in Chile:

- Scouting taught me basic first aid.

- On my mission we discovered a boy who had been severely cut by an ax and who was bleeding severely. I applied direct pressure and brought the boy to the hospital. The doctor told us we saved the boy's life.

A missionary serving in Anchorage, Alaska, told the following story in a letter sent to his parents:

> It was around 8 p.m., and my companion and I had just finished an appointment. We were about a one-hour walk from home, and decided to walk through a park in south Anchorage. Something didn't seem right; the sun was in our faces, and we couldn't see in front of us very well, but we both just felt like something was not right. Then we heard something unusual, so we shielded our eyes to see the source of the noise. Ten feet in front of us were two baby moose calves. By instinct we started to run the other way, but it was too late. The mother was already running at us from the other direction. To the left of us was a field of devil's club—huge plants with thorns—and on the right of us was a swamp. On the other side of the swamp was a play set that would get us off the ground and out of the way of the moose.
>
> We bolted as fast as we could through the swamp. It is really hard to run very fast when you sink up to your knees in mud. We barely made it to the top of the play set as the mother moose caught up to us. She rammed the play set repeatedly, and every few minutes she stood on her hind legs and tried to kick us. But we were up too high for her to reach us. She made a real mess of that play set. The moose would not leave. It started to get cold as the sun went down, and it started to rain. I knew that we had to keep moving the best we could up there to help us stay warm.
>
> We had been up on the play set for about two hours, and the mother moose showed no signs of leaving. As we sat

there on top of the play set we prayed. I thought about some of my Scouting experiences and things that I had learned during my Scouting years. I realized that several experiences that night called on skills I had learned in Scouting. First, I learned to always be aware of my surroundings. If we had not been paying attention, we would not have heard the calves and we probably would not have seen them in time to get away from their mother. We were able to assess the area quickly to know which way we should go. We didn't have a long time to decide anything—we just knew because of things that we had learned in Scouting. I also knew that as cold as it can get here in Alaska, we needed to stay warm by moving around. As I sat there thinking about all of that, it made me very grateful that I was an Eagle Scout and that I had a mother who would encourage me along. I was grateful for a dad that would take time off work and go on all the Scout trips with me.

We continued praying and around 10:30 p.m. a city worker showed up. He shot a gun in the air and scared away the moose. When he got to us he said, "Well, boys, where is your God now?" I looked at him and said, "He is watching over us. Why do you think you showed up when you did?"

A letter from a missionary in the New Jersey Newark Mission to his priests quorum/crew adviser in Arizona expressed a similar sentiment:

Venturing is a perfect stepping stone to missionary work. The best thing it teaches that helps in missionary work is self-accountability. We are out here responsible for ourselves. Nobody sets appointments for us. Nobody plans our days for us. Nobody checks our obedience. We are responsible for all of this ourselves. Thank you for all that you taught me while we were together.

A single parent mom, struggling to raise five children, recently forwarded to me an e-mail from her oldest son, serving a full-time mission in the Michigan Detroit Mission. She asked him in a previous e-mail, "did

Scouting help prepare you for your mission?" Here are some excerpts from his reply: "I definitely learned determination to overcome any obstacle and trial that came my way. When stepdad went to prison when I was sixteen, I could have given up and blamed my life on circumstances. But I chose to rise above my circumstances and become the person who I knew I could be. I had a goal to attend college and knew that I would have to work hard to be able to get into a good school, because we couldn't afford it ourselves. What I didn't know when I was 12, 14, or 16, that I now know that you knew Mom, was what I would learn while accomplishing my Scouting goals – character and integrity, a determination to overcome any obstacle and trial, but more importantly, a testimony of Jesus Christ and his gospel. It was the experiences of earning, not being given, my ranks and merit badges. I learned to make the Scout oath and law my personal oath and law to live by – my creed. I learned to make God my first priority. I said it every time I went for a Board of Review or had a Scout meeting. The principles that I have learned through the Scouting program have helped me every day of my life. If I hadn't learned the things I had and applied them, I guarantee that I would not be where or who I am today. It's because of those things that I learned as a Scout, that I'm currently serving as a missionary. It's the reason I am able to go to college and receive a full tuition scholarship. It's also the reason that I've been able to rise above my circumstances and not allow myself to lose focus of my potential as a child of God."

When properly carried out, Scouting can accelerate a young man's spiritual progression.

In a worldwide training meeting, Elder Richard G. Scott testified that the fundamental purpose of each auxiliary organization of the Church is to help plant and grow a testimony of the Savior Jesus Christ (see Richard G. Scott, "News of the Church," *Ensign,* March 2004, 74).

Scouting provides many opportunities to plant and grow a testimony of Jesus Christ. I like to use the word "accelerator." Growing up, most of us experienced major and minor accelerators that contributed to our spiritual growth: serving a full-time mission, attending a youth conference, enduring personal trials and tribulations, and so on. These experiences accelerated spiritual growth.

Scouting can provide various mini-accelerators, such as spiritually focused camping trips. A Scouter in California shared with me how he did this:

Our annual priests quorum four-day, three-night summer camping trip included early-morning scripture study
and nightly campfires with a gospel theme. One night the
young men were given a letter written by their fathers in
advance; the letters were an expression of love for their
sons. The Holy Ghost was there. You don't find any greater
reverence anyplace than what we had. We ended the final
evening with a testimony meeting and a kneeling prayer.
Several boys in their testimonies commented on reading the
scriptures each day. Oh, and the whitewater rafting. You
know, that's the excuse to take these boys away for a few
days (without their electronic games or music devices) so
we can peel back the worldly layers and get to their hearts.

An excerpt from a talk given by a Bishop in Lindon, Utah, illustrates
how several mini-accelerators helped him come to know the joy of serving
in the Church as a young man, and that the work in which he was engaged
was true.

In 1979 after completing the mile swim in summer camp
in Arizona, I felt strong and capable. After a week at camp
we had a final troop campfire and all bore their testimonies. *I knew then.*

In 1980 while earning the Environmental Science
merit badge in Arkansas, I appreciated nature for the first
time and felt closer to my Heavenly Father. *I knew then.*

In 1980 when my Scoutmaster told stories about his
service in Vietnam and shared his witness of the Lord's
protection of him and his men, I felt the Spirit very
strongly. *I knew then.*

In 1981 while on a six-day canoe trip our supply canoe capsized on the second day and we lost half of our
food in the river. Our Scoutmaster knelt and prayed with
us that we would have enough food to finish the trip. We
not only ate, we ate well. I saw that my Scoutmaster trusted the Lord and that prayers were answered. *I knew then.*

In 1983 our Explorer post went on a backpacking
trip. After eight days, mostly rainy ones, with water-

logged packs, blisters, and mosquito bites, we went home as young men who had conquered an incredible task. I learned self-reliance, preparedness, and teamwork. *I knew then.*

In 1984 we had youth conference with three surrounding stakes. The activities were a lot of fun and being around girls was exciting, but the final testimony meeting was a spiritual pinnacle for me. The talks given by our leaders and the testimonies we bore as a group brought the witness of the Spirit more powerfully than I had ever felt before. I learned that my leaders loved me, that we were all in this together, and that my testimony mattered and could strengthen those around me. *I knew then.*

In 1985 when I graduated from seminary and high school with a firm conviction of who I was and what I believed in, I finally realized that many of my leaders over the years had made a significant difference in my life. *I knew then.*

When I went on a mission and taught the gospel to the people of Montana, I learned to love others and to lead by example. I learned what the Lord expected from me, and committed that I would do it. *I knew then.*

When I was married in the Salt Lake Temple to my sweetheart, my joy was so full. I wanted to do all that was required of me to be with her for eternity. *I knew then.*

When we had our first child, I wanted him to have every opportunity I had been given as a child raised in the Church. I wanted him to know what I know, and to have his own conviction. *I knew then.*

Testimonies are fragile. In the mission field I learned that when we left the home of an investigator, Satan immediately entered the home and tried to dissuade that investigator. In many ways young men are like investigators; they need constant, regular opportunities to strengthen their testimonies. The *Preach My Gospel* manual states, "One of the best ways to help people make and keep commitments is to extend a commitment invitation" (p. 196). The manual explains that a commitment invitation is often a "will you" question, and it requires a *yes* or *no* response. "Invitations should be specific, direct and clear. They invite or lead people to decide on a course of action" (p. 197). The manual then provides several examples of "will you" questions. I suggest you use this commitment pattern with your young men to help them commit to make and keep sacred covenants. Scouting, if implemented properly, can provide an ideal environment to generate this kind of commitment.

Chapter 11: Traditions of our Fathers

In *Fiddler on the Roof*, Tevya said, "You may ask, 'How did this tradition get started?' I'll tell you—I don't know, but it's a tradition."

Regardless of how they get started, it is good for wards to create lasting traditions that young people can anticipate. I have seen many good traditions in Scouting. Troop 114 of Littleton, Colorado, recited the Scout Law each week forwards and backwards. Many troops have traditional camping locations, a special service project they do each year, or special ceremonies unique to them. A Venturing crew in Arizona had a special pancake breakfast once a month at 6 a.m. at the adviser's home; the adviser made some kind of special sauce to put on the pancakes and they had inspirational speakers. According to one of the young men, this was an event not to be missed.

But traditions aren't always positive. The prophet Alma, speaking of the Lamanites, said, "it is because of the traditions of their fathers that caused them to remain in their state of ignorance . . ." (Alma 9:16). We sometimes unknowingly create and foster traditions that are destructive to our youth. Most LDS adult leaders were Scouts as youth, but many had a Scouting experience that was much less than the ideal. Because of this many of our Aaronic Priesthood leaders have never witnessed a properly functioning Boy Scout troop. When called to serve, they tend to run a program similar to what they experienced as young people. Out of ignorance and without intending to do any harm, they carry bad traditions to the next generation.

The German psychologist Max Ringelman identified a phenomenon known as *social loafing* (see J. M. Jackson and S. G. Harkins, "Equity in Effort; An Explanation of the Social Loafing Effect," *Journal of Personality and Social Psychology*, 49[1985]:1199–1206). He noticed that as increasingly more people were added to a group that was pulling on a rope, the total force exerted by the group rose, but the average force exerted by each group member declined. A knowledgeable Scouter in a ward can intimidate others because of his/her experience, causing other leaders to sit back and be social loafers. They may tell themselves, "John is the Scouter. He will attend roundtables, he will pick up the awards at the Scout office, and so on." By the way, what is a "Scouter"? Most often, a Scouter is an adult that served as a Scoutmaster many years ago, now serves as a commissioner, and may or may not administer Scouting properly. I have learned that tenure in Scouting, number of patches on the uniform, etc. is not a guarantee of successful Scouting.

A Scout leader in Utah shared the following story with me:

> "Scouting is stupid!" my fifteen-year-old son replied when I encouraged him to finish up a few merit badges, complete his Eagle Rank, and continue to work on his Duty to God award.
>
> "What do you mean?" I asked. "Didn't you like the river trip we just completed—the forty rapids you were able to row, the five-mile hike to Indian Ruins, swimming, fishing, and camping for six days?"
>
> "Well, yes, that was really fun," my son replied.
>
> "Well, I'm sorry to let you in on a secret, son, but that was Scouting. The priesthood blessing given streamside, the evening testimony meeting, and the spiritual thoughts each day—those were all Scouting."
>
> "Dad that is not how we have done Scouting in our ward. Scouting is checking off the boxes as fast as you can so you can earn twelve merit badges at camp."
>
> "Sorry, son, if that's how you see it; that's not what Scouting is at all. Some boys may get through the program swiftly, but in so doing, they might be missing opportunities to really get to know great men who have a common interest with them. The only ones being shortchanged are the boys who see this as a race to Eagle.
>
> "Scouting provides you an opportunity to get to know sage men and women who have specific skills, but more importantly, men and women who will share their

testimony and values with you, so that you can be well-prepared for life. That is what Scouting is all about."

My son did not know what to say, yet his comment— "Scouting is stupid!"—rang loudly through my ears all evening long.

This young man's perception of Scouting was etched into his mind by a pervasive trend in the Church to follow the tradition of the previous scouting leaders. Destructive traditions usually begin innocently. Remember when you received that big box of supplies from the previous leader? When the released leader gives his "stuff" to the newly called leader, there is a tendency for the new person to think that he has to fulfill the calling exactly as his predecessor did. But you bring your unique personality and experience into your callings. You can learn much from the experience and perspective of those who proceed you, but you must seek inspiration from the Lord and get officially trained by the Church and Scouting if you're going to avoid fostering bad traditions.

Ineffective traditions include focusing only on advancement, focusing on entertaining the youth, taking the path of least resistance, starting mutual fifteen minutes late, gravitating towards the gym to play basketball because nothing else is planned, and approaching callings casually. Destructive traditions include paint-balling (and calling it an Aaronic Priesthood activity because it is not authorized in Scouting) or playing video games on mutual night, refusing to attend Scout training and Roundtable, and failing to create a Scout committee.

If you have inherited any of these traditions, or others that weaken the effectiveness of the Scouting program in your ward, you can break the cycle and bless the lives of present and future young men. In his book, *Leading Change,* James O'Toole suggests we "abandon the tyranny of custom . . . by building an alternative system of belief and allowing others to adopt it as their own" (O'Toole, 1996). Remember the watershed questions Elder Bednar suggested that we use to measure all our activities: Are we strengthening belief in Christ? Are we strengthening the family?

Here's how one dedicated adult leader overcame the traditions of a poor program in a ward:

> When I came to the priests quorum nine years ago, they
> had no program other than the occasional basketball

game. There was no calendar; there were no presidency meetings with the priests, and hence little quorum brotherhood or progress. Our young men were enjoying a tremendous Scouting experience from ages twelve through fifteen, then at age sixteen they were losing the momentum they had experienced in those early years.

We developed a program based on the Aaronic Priesthood purposes and Venturing and a theme of "Serve Hard, Work Hard, and Play Hard," in that order, under the direction of the bishop. On our first high adventure we had only me, one other leader, and two young men. It was a bit discouraging, somewhat like trying to lift a sleeping elephant.

We continued working with our new small nucleus of young men, training the new quorum presidency how to effectively develop and run a program with high-quality career nights, missionary preparation, outdoor high adventure, physical fitness, meaningful service activities, and occasional social events with the Laurels. Within fourteen months we had an average attendance on Tuesday nights of eleven of the sixteen priests. These young men began leaving for missions and were better prepared to serve.

To avoid creating bad traditions and fostering existing bad traditions, answer these four questions to see how you are doing:

1. Do I utilize BSA resources?

A Scout leader from Meridian, Idaho, shared with me the following metaphor:

We have Scout leaders with machetes trying to create their own path (program), cutting down trees and bushes, trying to create a path from scratch, when a few feet away lies a well-maintained, paved path created by the Boy Scouts of America, with specific directions on how to run the program.

In January of 2010, the Young Men General Presidency wrote," The Church of Jesus Christ of Latter-day Saints desires all Scouting leaders to receive the training necessary for their individual position. We must find ways to help each adult who works with Young Men to have a desire to become fully trained. If we are going to be able to provide a dynamic Aaronic Priesthood activity program that develops them spiritually, creates strong brotherhood, provides wide opportunity for service to others, and reaches out to all young men, we must be better prepared to use the tools of Scouting through proper understanding. That understanding only comes through effective training and proper implementation."

Immediately after the call to serve, Scouting leaders need to attend leader-specific training for their positions. And, as soon as possible, sign up for Woodbadge. Woodbadge is one of the key factors in helping LDS leaders see the big picture. A new leader should plan on attending district roundtable each month. A habit of not attending roundtable will immediately handicap your Scouting program; you will be out of the loop regarding upcoming activities that could greatly enhance your program. A roundtable should not be viewed as just another meeting to attend; instead, you should look forward to finding specific solutions to problems at roundtable.

I received an e-mail from a member of a stake presidency asking about roundtable attendance:

> I am a counselor in the stake presidency and the co-chairman for the District LDS Relationship Committee. We have six stakes in our district. Our six stakes have made some significant progress in providing more stake leaders to serve in district leadership positions, including roundtable commissioners. At our last LDS relationship meeting, we discussed roundtable attendance and we ran into a small controversy. We'd like to know your counsel with regards to roundtable attendance.
>
> We have received counsel that our Young Men and Scout leaders need to be trained. All six of the stake presidencies strongly agree with this counsel. However, we have also been counseled to not put too much burden on the family. We want our Young Men and Scout leaders to come to roundtable as often as possible, but we also do not want to put too much burden on their time. Because of that concern a couple of stakes are thinking of encouraging their

Young Men leaders to come as often as possible, with a requirement of at least once a quarter. I am not sure exactly what counsel to give the leaders of our stake.

This is how I responded to him, and this response has universal application: "Monthly roundtable attendance is critical to conducting a successful Scouting program. The purpose of roundtable is to train, inform, and motivate. Units that miss roundtable find themselves outside the loop related to district and council activities. Roundtable is essentially "in-service" training for LDS Scouting leaders. Roundtable is no more of a burden than attending a stake priesthood leadership meeting. The Church delegates this training to the Boy Scouts of America. Some stakes provide quarterly auxiliary training also.

It's great that LDS Scouters are getting involved on the district and council levels. This should help make a more quality roundtable and make it time well spent.

We need to be sensitive to not burden families, but Aaronic Priesthood/ Scouting leaders in the Church should commit to monthly roundtable attendance at the time of the call. Scouting is a tool to help bring young men to Christ. Roundtable attendance is a key to successful Scouting in a ward and stake."

Soon after the call to serve, a Scout leader should purchase the Scouting literature needed to fulfill the position, read it from cover to cover, and implement it. This sounds so simple, but is rarely done. Cub Scout leaders should obtain the *Cub Scout Leader Book*, Boy Scout Leaders should get the *Scoutmaster Handbook* and *Boy Scout Handbook,* Varsity Scout leaders should get the *Varsity Scout Guidebook,* and Venturing Leaders should obtain the *Venturing Leader Manual.* I promise you that attending leader-specific training, attending Woodbadge, attending monthly roundtables, participating in council and district activities, and reading and applying the information in the Scouting literature will transform your ward Scouting program into a vibrant one.

2.   Does my ward have a Scout committee?

A common complaint I hear from Scoutmasters is this: "I'm burned out— I'm doing everything." Often the problem is the Scoutmaster's inability to ask for help or the ward leadership's failure to get help. The Scoutmaster/ Varsity Coach/Venturing adviser's principal role is to work directly with the young men, to minister to them and teach them how to lead.

Sometimes Scout leaders get unnecessarily caught up in administration (such as handling the awards, transportation, equipment, and so on).

In most wards the Scout Committee consists of committee members, the unit leaders (Scoutmaster, Varsity coach, and Venturing adviser), and the Primary president. Committee members are parents of young men and others called by the bishopric. The *LDS Scouting Handbook* instructs that qualified adults—regardless of whether they are members of the Church—including fathers and mothers of boys and young men may serve on the committee (see p. 3).

The purpose of the Scout committee is to take the administrative load off the Scout leader and disseminate it among committee members—the committee chair, treasurer, secretary, transportation chair, equipment chair, and advancement chair. The unit leaders represent their unit and quorum to the committee. In the Scoutmaster's case, he represents the patrol leaders' council, asking the committee to assist and support the plans of the troop. The committee can help units stay strong and provide continuity during the times in between leaders. Each month the committee meets, under the direction of the committee chair. The committee chair need not be a "boy's man," but he or she should be an organizer of adults.

I met a dynamic Scout committee chair recently in Arizona. She was a blessing to her ward's Scouting program, taking on all the administrative duties, freeing up the Scouting unit leaders to work with the young men. If the Scoutmaster is empowered to concentrate his efforts on ministering to the young men and the administrative burden is minimized, young men in the troop can be blessed with an inspired, focused leader.

3. Do I take my calling seriously?

In Search of Excellence makes the point that the best predictor of a project's failure or success was whether people volunteered or had been assigned to the project (see Peters and Waterman, *In Search of Excellence* [New York: Warner Books, 1984], 203).

Because we are called and don't volunteer in the Church, we have a tendency to approach our callings in a casual way. One of the assignments I give students at Brigham Young University is to attend a nearby Scout troop and write a report about it. I suggest that the students choose a chapel on a Tuesday, Wednesday, or Thursday night, walk in unannounced around 7 p.m., and observe. Each student then completes a worksheet and answers questions. Here are the questions and some sample responses:

IN YOUR OPINION, WAS THE MEETING ORGANIZED AND RUN WELL?

—"Not really. They had an opening ceremony, then went to the gym and played basketball."

—"It was sad to see that the Scoutmaster did not show up on time; he was thirty minutes late. The boys sat around for ten minutes, then the Young Men president showed up and started them on the First Aid merit badge."

—"Yes, there were a lot of things to do. It ran like a well-oiled machine and it was organized and fun."

—"It was a little messy to start out, but by the end they had it under control."

—"The meeting started at 7 p.m., but was over pretty quickly. Before 7:30 everyone was gone."

—"Yes, the youth leader started off the meeting by calling on different boys to tie the timber hitch, double half hitch, etc."

—"No, there was no structure to the meeting and no control. The adult leader did not have anything planned and the boys didn't care anymore."

—"No, the leaders showed up late. The leader who planned the activity gave some papers to a boy and told him to teach it to the others, then he left."

—"They were working on the Camping merit badge during the meeting. They started the meeting with the Scout Oath, Law, Motto, and Slogan. They had seven boys and they seemed to be interested. The meeting ran well and seemed to be well organized. Afterwards they played a game called 'Steal the Bacon.'"

DID THE MEETING HAVE EVIDENCE OF BEING PLANNED AND RUN BY THE YOUTH?

—"The Scoutmaster tried to get the Scouts to do a merit badge, but couldn't control them, so they played basketball."

—"Yes, the SPL took over and he knew how to do everything. They had a uniform inspection. Then they turned the time over to the leader to teach camping skills."

—"The SPL was trying to run the meeting, but the Scoutmaster kept interfering."

—"The boys helped each other tie knots and lash. They were really excited at the end because they lashed together a thing and it withstood the weight of all of us standing on it."

—"Unfortunately not, unless you count the boys deciding to go in the gym and leave the Scoutmaster behind. The Scoutmaster said and did everything; the boys were bored."

—"The meeting was run by the youth because no leaders were there for half of the meeting."

In June 2006 a survey was conducted by the National Council of the Boy Scouts of America. Survey forms were sent randomly to 3,000 Cub Scout leaders throughout the country. The national council wanted to know about training and tenure of Cub Scout leaders. This was not a survey targeted to LDS Cub Scout leaders, but the following responses reveal attitudes from LDS leaders.

—"It's just a church assignment I was called to do. I don't think I need training." (This sentiment was expressed twenty-seven times in different ways.)

—"Church calling—won't be here that long. No need to get any training—just filling in for the time being." (This sentiment was expressed fifteen times in different ways.)

—"It's a church calling, and unless I'm released, then I plan on being a den leader this time next year. But I finally know what I am doing, so they will probably release me soon (it always happens that way)."

—"They probably won't release me, so I guess I'm stuck."

—"I was a Cub Scout as a kid, and was an Eagle by age fourteen, and I'm a returned missionary. I think I can handle it without anyone 'training' me."

What is the source of these attitudes? In the April 2007 general conference, Elder Henry B. Eyring pointed out that complacency can affect any of us—even adults with rich experience. The better and longer we serve, the more the adversary will try to convince us that we have earned a rest, have sacrificed enough, have worked long and hard—and that it's time to give someone else a chance (see "This Day," *Ensign*, May 2007, 89–91).

4. Is the scope and importance of the call communicated at the time it is issued?

Administering the Church states that "soon after being sustained, every new leader should receive an orientation about the calling". (Book 2,

2010, pg.14) I have served in five bishoprics and understand the urgency sometimes connected with calling people to serve in the Church. I remember feeling pressure from auxiliary leaders to call people to serve, and I was occasionally guilty of being more concerned with getting a quick "yes" than taking the time to orient the person being called.

I'm convinced that time spent training and orienting newly called Aaronic Priesthood/Scouting leaders is time well spent. At the time of the call, the member of the bishopric should convey a realistic assessment of the time needed and the training required. The spouse should be present and have input during the meeting. The date and location of the next training session should be given to the new person. Scouting leaders should know when they are called that they are expected to go camping monthly and to spend a week at summer camp. The one making the call should impress on the new leader the goals of strengthening testimonies and bringing young men to Christ.

An experienced LDS adult advisor from California shared with me the five things a Bishopric member should do when issuing a call to serve with the young men;

1. Give the person an adult registration form
2. Give the book or manual appropriate for the calling
3. Encouragement to get a uniform
4. A flyer or brochure about the upcoming training session.
5. Information about the date and location of the monthly Roundtable meeting

According to the *LDS Scouting Handbook,* the men who are called as deacons, teachers, and priests quorum advisers also serve as the Young Men's presidency in the ward. These same three men also serve as Scoutmaster, Varsity coach, and Venturing crew adviser (see p. 3). All of these, of course, should be surrounded by good assistants. In this way, the quorum adviser, member of the Young Men's presidency, and Scouting unit leader are the same person. There's a good reason for doing it this way: if the deacons quorum adviser and Scoutmaster are two different men, it is unlikely that they will be completely united and focused on the same priorities. In the best situations, young men enjoy consistency in adult leadership.

Chapter 12: Challenges

All of us face challenges, real or perceived, in magnifying our callings. Several challenges have already been addressed in this book. I'd like to address four other challenges facing LDS Scout leaders that are common potential roadblocks to a successful Aaronic Priesthood and Scouting program.

THE CHALLENGE OF PERCEPTION

Many times I have heard LDS Scout leaders say that they weren't going to invest much into their calling because it was just a matter of time before the Church withdrew from Scouting. They base their prediction on events that have occurred on the national level in recent years.

On June 28, 2000, the U.S. Supreme Court settled *Boys Scouts of America v James Dale*, ruling by a five-to-four margin that the Boy Scouts have the constitutional right to exclude avowed homosexuals from Scouting (see www.bsa–discrimination.org/html/dale–top.html). The decision was a decisive legal victory for the Scouts, but on a public relations level, it was a nightmare that divided and polarized the nation. Most religious organizations lined up behind Scouting. However, some PTAs, United Way boards, and some major corporations publicly announced that they were cutting funds and/or access to Boy Scout councils and units.

The Supreme Court case and the introduction by the LDS Church of the Fulfilling Your Duty to God program in 2001 caused many members of the Church to believe that the Boy Scouts of America and the LDS Church were planning to part ways. The Fulfilling Your Duty to God program appeared to be a potential replacement for Scouting, as a hedge against a time when the Scouting program might disappear.

As I traveled around the country giving presentations to LDS audiences, I was often asked, "When [not if] the Church leaves Scouting, how will the

Church's departure affect the Boy Scouts of America?" The Young Men's General President of the Church at the time, Elder Melvin Hammond, was overwhelmed by phone calls from LDS leaders around the country expressing the same concern.

Elder Hammond was active on the National Board of the Boy Scouts of America. He was also appointed to serve on a key committee with other prominent Church and civic leaders to clarify the Boy Scouts' position on gays and atheists requesting membership in Scouting. The committee concluded with a resolution, which Elder Hammond supported, that simply stated, "We still support emphatically the timeless values of Scouting. If there are councils that want to violate those timeless values then, in effect, we just will not charter them. We won't renew their charter" ("Scouting's Future," *Church News,* Sept. 20, 2003).

At that point Elder Hammond determined that he needed to communicate with the general Church populace about the current relationship between the LDS Church and the Boy Scouts of America. *Church News* reporter Jason Swensen asked Elder Hammond, "Can you comment on the ongoing relationship between the Church and the Scouting program?" Elder Hammond answered, "I think there's no question that at this period of time the relationship between the Church and Scouting is on solid ground. . . ." The reporter then asked, "There are rumors that the Church is planning to part ways with the Scouting program. Can you address that?" Elder Hammond replied, "It's pure rumor. I think the rumor arose out of the creation and implementation of the [Church's Aaronic Priesthood] Duty to God program. The Duty to God program was not meant in any way to diminish Scouting in the Church. It was meant to complement Scouting and they work hand-in-hand beautifully" (*ibid.*).

In the decade since the article in the *Church News,* Scouting in the LDS Church flourished, and the relationship between the Boy Scouts of America and the LDS Church was magnified. Through the efforts of President Charles W. Dahlquist, President David L. Beck, and their presidencies, Woodbadge attendance doubled since 2003 and due to demand, Philmont offers two weeks of LDS Priesthood leader training.

THE CHALLENGE OF SMALL QUORUMS
Outside the LDS Church all young men ages eleven to eighteen are in one troop, with older boys giving leadership to younger boys. It usually works well, and is considered the model for a successful troop. But in the LDS

Church we have quorums and priesthood keys that require a different model for organizing the troop leadership. To serve young men ages twelve to eighteen, each ward should have a Boy Scout troop, a Varsity Scout team, and a Venturing crew, even if the respective quorums are small.

For young men in the Aaronic Priesthood it is important to maintain quorum identity. All quorums should meet separately on Sunday to help maintain identity and to recognize and honor priesthood keys. When quorums combine regularly, the priesthood keys are diluted or ignored altogether, and the purposes of the Aaronic Priesthood are frustrated. The quorums may combine occasionally on mutual nights. *Administering the Church* says that" Where there are few young men, a Scout troop may be organized to serve multiple wards and branches, or, in some instances, an entire stake or district..." (Book 2, 2010, pg. 59) And for quorum meetings on Sunday with few young men, "quorums may meet together for instruction. Even when quorums meet together, separate quorums should be organized, with leaders called and sustained for each quorum. When possible, each quorum should begin to meet separately and should have a full presidency and a secretary...If quorums meet together, the priest quorum assistants, teachers quorum president, and deacons quorum president take turns conducting." (Book 2, 2010, pg. 57)

In a large Scouting training session in Rexburg, Idaho, I shared the challenge of small quorums. Several brethren complained about how hard it is to run a viable Scouting/Aaronic Priesthood program with only two or three young men in a quorum. Then in the back of the room a timid hand was raised. The man had tears in his eyes. He told us the following story:

> I was a fifteen-year-old deacon and had been less active for more than a year. One day a man came to my home. He pulled up in a 280Z and asked to talk to me. He told me and my parents that he was my teachers quorum adviser, and I was one of only three teachers in the ward.
>
> I loved cars and was especially fond of his car. Over the next several months he came to my home often; we worked on his car together with my dad and went to some races. He remembered me on my birthday. Gradually I began attending Church. I was ordained a teacher and at age sixteen was ordained a priest. This man later

became my bishop and then my stake president. I owe my life to him. Without him I would not be here today. If I had been in a large quorum, it would have been easier to forget about me.

Brethren, never complain about small quorums—they give leaders a chance to get to know the young men better.

President Henry B. Eyring has told of his own experience growing up in a branch with small quorums. When he was ordained a deacon, his was the only family in the branch. They had no chapel; the branch met in his house. He was the only deacon, and his brother was the only teacher. Reflecting on that experience, he said he has learned that a quorum's strength does not come from numbers, or even the age and maturity of its members; instead, it comes from how united in righteousness the quorum members are (see "A Priesthood Quorum," *Ensign,* Nov. 2006, 3).

THE CHALLENGE OF FINANCES

A common challenge for LDS Scouting units is the unit budget allowance. I'm surprised to find that most LDS leaders do not know how much money they have to spend; most say that they've been told to minimize expenses, but don't know exactly how much they have been given. This creates a "poverty complex" among our adult leaders that translates into a poor program for youth.

In my service as a bishop in Texas, we held a ward council meeting each November to review and approve the ward budget. Each auxiliary leader was given a copy of the entire ward budget that showed how much money each group was receiving. We reminded the leaders to spend their entire allotment and to spend it wisely.

Most questions about budget allowance can be answered by examining the Church's guidelines for funding youth activities found in *Administering the Church,* Book 2, 2010, pgs. 59, 103,107) .

1. Funding for Aaronic Priesthood activities, including Scouting activities... should come from the ward budget.
2. If the ward budget does not have sufficient funds to pay for an annual extended Scout camp or similar activity for young men, leaders may ask participants to pay for part or all of it.
3. If funds from participants are not sufficient, the bishop may authorize one group fund-raising activity annually that complies with the guidelines.

4. In no case should the expenses or travel for an annual camp or similar activity be excessive. Nor should the lack of personal funds prohibit a member from participating.
5. Equipment and supplies are purchased with ward budget funds. If these funds are not sufficient, the bishop may authorize one group fund-raising activity annually that complies with the guidelines.

Many wards skip #2 and move directly from #1 (the ward budget allowance) to #3 (fund-raisers). Doing so fails our youth in an important way. Some wards have initiated opportunities for young men to individually earn their own way through doing yard work, special projects, and so on. Emphasizing a young man's ability to pay his own way builds self-reliance that will carry over into adulthood. If we're not careful, a young man can glide through six years of Aaronic Priesthood and Scouting activities with no personal investment or ownership.

In a letter dated April 6, 2004, the Presiding Bishopric of the Church announced that the annual budget allowance has been increased to include the current $48 per person attending sacrament meeting plus $50 per youth ages twelve through seventeen attending Young Men and Young Women meetings.

The Church, recognizing the need to provide meaningful activities for the youth, has invested a considerable sum in our youth programs. Unfortunately, most Scout leaders I share this information with are unaware of the $50 increase and are implementing programs under the previous policy.

Food for activities is another challenge that affects the budget allowance. The Church guidelines say that wards should generally use the budget to pay for food for activities. While potluck-type activities can be held, the guidelines say, these should not place undue burdens on members (see *Administering the Church,* 2010, pgs. 103-104).

A monthly campout can be considered a "potluck-type" activity. Each boy attending the campout can be assigned to bring a portion of the meal, which reduces pressure on the ward budget and contributes to the young man's self-reliance. This approach also builds teamwork.

Scouting leaders that use the BSA adult surveys can uncover resources in their ward to help save money on activities and provide a more varied program. Boy Scout troops should use the Troop Resource Survey, Varsity teams should use the Varsity Scout Resource Survey, and Venturing crews use the Program Capability Interest Survey.

Remember to follow the counsel of your Stake President and Bishop as it relates to budget allowance guidelines. With knowledge of the budget allowance process, regular dialogue with priesthood leadership, and careful allocation of sacred funds, we can avoid "poverty complex" and provide a program that meets the needs of our young men.

THE CHALLENGE OF DISTRACTIONS

On mutual night our young men have two significant distractions: sports and girls. While attempting to do Scouting in the Scout room, the young men often hear the muffled bouncing of the ball in the cultural hall and the shrill sounds of the young women in the hallway.

It's difficult to run effective programs when at least six groups— Beehives, Mia Maids, Laurels, Scouts, Varsity Scouts, and Venturers—are competing for space and time. Often we also compete for space with the Cub Scouts and the Relief Society. And in many parts of the country, two wards meet at the same building on the same night, resulting in twelve groups that are competing for space.

We can learn much from observing the way other churches implement Scouting. I have visited dozens of Catholic and Protestant churches on Scout night. No girls are present, and in most cases no basketball court exists. These troops have uninterrupted time to concentrate on Scouting.

But what can we do to address these distractions? We can't tear down the basketball hoops or tell the young women to go home. Part of the solution lies in our attitude toward our meetinghouse. After opening exercises on mutual night, many successful troops, teams, and crews leave the building and conduct their activities elsewhere, usually close to the building. I have seen LDS troops meeting in heated barns and in elementary schools across the street from the meetinghouse. In both instances the troops succeeded in keeping the undivided attention of twelve- to thirteen-year-old boys. I know of many Varsity teams and Venturing crews that often meet outside the church building.

Chapter 13: Paradigm Shift

"The word *paradigm* stems from the Greek word *paradeigma,* originally a scientific term but commonly used today to mean a perception, assumption, theory, frame of reference, or lens through which one views the world. It's like a map of a territory or city. If inaccurate, it will make no difference how hard you try to find your destination or how positively you think—you'll stay lost" (Stephen R. Covey, *The Leader of the Future,* "Leading in the Knowledge Worker Age" [San Francisco: Jossey–Bass, 2006]), 220).

Most LDS Scouting leaders were Scouts as youth. Many may have experienced substandard programs and carry on the substandard program (paradigm) as adult leaders. Throughout the Church we need a seismic shift in the way we approach Scouting in our Aaronic Priesthood quorums.

PARADIGM SHIFT FOR ADULT LEADERS

A stake president told me a powerful story of his paradigm shift:

> Many years ago, I served as a Varsity coach. I had a bad attitude about my calling, refused to attend Scout training, and attended meetings just to keep a dedicated Scouter in the stake from 'bugging' me. One day I noticed that the young men in my quorum were acting the same way—feeling forced to do service projects and only coming to meetings because their mothers made them come. I repented, went to Scout training, and began to focus on the young men. I have discovered over the years that the Spirit will not work with you if you are negative and approach your calling with the wrong motivations. After I repented, the Spirit directed me in ways to help bring the young men to Christ through Scouting.

With a seismic shift in attitude, this priesthood leader has over the years positively influenced the lives of hundreds of young men. He was recently asked to direct a Woodbadge course in his Boy Scout council.

The following suggestions for Aaronic Priesthood advisers will help create a paradigm shift in the way we approach Scouting in the Church, help bring young men to Christ, and summarize the key points in this book.

1. Implement Elder David A. Bednar's challenge.
Plan and evaluate all activities and associations with young men through the following lens:
- What are we doing to foster faith in Jesus Christ?

- What are we doing to strengthen the family?

2. Commit to memory the Boy Scout aims and methods. Plan and evaluate all activities and associations with young men with those aims and methods in mind.

3. Remember: advancement is only one of the methods. Make sure you implement the other methods as well.

4. Read the Boy Scout literature appropriate for your calling.

5. Get trained by the Boy Scouts of America, completing:
Youth Protection Training
Fast Start Training
This is Scouting
Leader-Specific Training
Woodbadge

6. Develop the habit and tradition of conducting a reflection at the conclusion of each activity.

7. Abide by the following:
Adult Adviser Oath
On my honor I will do my best to train young men how to lead; stand back and be a shadow leader; have a finely tuned spiritual antenna; and recognize priesthood keys.

Adult Adviser Slogan
Never do for a young man what he can do for himself.

8. Stop doing some of the things you may be doing now:
   • Stop thinking of Scouting as nothing more than checking off boxes and earning badges.
   • Stop thinking of your calling as merely finding ways to entertain young men.
   • Stop promoting "puppet leadership."
   • Stop fostering traditions that are spiritually destructive to young men.

PARADIGM SHIFT FOR PARENTS

Parents play a major role in the success of Scouting in a ward. They should be involved in and connected with their son's Aaronic Priesthood quorum and Scouting activities. I suggest that parents adopt the following practices:

1. Recognize the spiritual dimension of Scouting. Ask your son when he returns from activities what was discussed that strengthened his spirituality. Be as concerned about your son's spiritual progress as you are about his advancement progress. Expect that your son will return from camping trips with a stronger testimony of the gospel.

   I asked a male BYU student to help me put up a poster in the Wilkinson Center at BYU. Afterwards I told him that he had done his "good deed for the day." I asked if he had been a Boy Scout. He replied, "Yes." When I asked if he was an Eagle Scout, he replied, "My Mom was!"

2. Prepare your sons to lead in their Aaronic Priesthood quorums. Support them when they are called to a formal position.

3. Memorize the Scout Oath, Law, Motto, and Slogan and the Aaronic Priesthood purposes. Incorporate them into your family home evenings and discussions.

4. Recognize and utilize all the tools available to help your son in his Aaronic Priesthood years. These tools include the *For the Strength*

of Youth pamphlet, *Preach My Gospel,* the Duty to God program (much of which should be completed at home), and Scouting.

I have talked with many mothers who told me that for them, Scouting was simply sewing on badges, smelling firewood smoke in the home, and laundering dirty clothes after a campout. When I introduced them to the spiritual dimension of Scouting, each of these sisters said, "I wish I had known. . . ."

Had these sisters been aware of the potential of Scouting to contribute to their son's spiritual growth, each patch they sewed on their son's uniform or sash would have evoked memories of spiritual insights gained and shared. Instead of anticipating only the temporal chores that awaited them upon their son's return from camp, they would have sent him off anticipating the spiritual discussions they might have when he returned.

When a young man "graduates" from the Aaronic Priesthood, he should have attained several competencies that will prepare him to receive the Melchizedek Priesthood, receive temple ordinances, fulfill an honorable full-time mission, and be a righteous husband and father. As he enters the bishop's office for his Melchizedek Priesthood interview, he should have several "spiritual badges" engraved on his heart in addition to the physical badges on his merit badge sash:

- Appreciation of Serving Others merit badge

- Strong Work Ethic merit badge

- Loving the Scriptures merit badge

- Practical Leadership Experience merit badge

- Meaningful Prayer merit badge

- Spiritual Experiences merit badge

Our focus as advisers and parents should be on helping Aaronic Priesthood holders earn these "spiritual merit badges." The activity arm of the Aaronic Priesthood is designed to help young men attain these qualities and experiences.

That one spiritually focused campout, that one reflection, that one conversation on the trail, that one service project at the widow's home . . . these are all small but significant things that could alter the course of a young man's life.

On a windy summer day many years ago, my family was eating lunch in our camper on the Oregon coast highway. I was ten years old. We had spent a fun day exploring the tide pools and hiking along the coastline. Below the highway on the rugged coastline was a twenty-foot-wide and a hundred-yard-long opening in the basalt shoreline called the Devil's Churn. The fury of the Pacific Ocean boils through the churn with large, foaming waves, sending the water flying into the air like a geyser as it crashes against the rocks. The water is cold and deep, and the rock walls are jagged.

A frantic knock on the camper door interrupted our meal. A young man announced that his girlfriend had fallen in the churn. My dad quickly grabbed a rope and my mother found a blanket. We ran down the trail to the churn. There, bobbing in the churn, was a young woman. Minutes earlier she had reached over to get a starfish and was swept into the churn by a wave. Her boyfriend had thrown her the life buoy provided on the shore, but he had failed to hold on to the rope attached to the other end. Every few seconds she was lifted ten feet or so by a wave rushing through the churn. Every wave threatened to cast her into the jagged rocks. My dad tied a bowline knot and threw it out to the helpless woman.

There was no time to spare; the cold water would eventually induce hypothermia. Her strength and body temperature were slowly slipping away. She could not climb up the steep rock walls by herself; she needed assistance. After several attempts to get the rope to her, we managed to lift her up across the jagged rocks to safety. She was cold, wet, and scraped up, but she was alive and very grateful. She hugged my dad while my mother put a warm blanket around her.

This story has application for young men in today's world. In the last days "shall he [Satan] rage in the hearts of the children of men, and stir them up to anger against that which is good. And others will he pacify, and lull them away into carnal security, that they will say: All is well in Zion . . . and thus the devil cheateth their souls, and leadeth them away carefully down to hell" (2 Ne. 28:20–21).

Too many of our young men are falling into a churn of worldliness and are being "carefully led down to hell." The large waves of the world are crashing over their heads, and the cold carnal security is slowly, carefully sapping their spirits into a hypothermic state.

Scouting can be the rope, the lifeline. To all of us involved in Scouting—parents and leaders alike—YOU are the person on the shore throwing the lifeline, making a spiritual connection, connecting the young man to Christ—the only One who can save him. Is your rope strong enough? Will the knot hold?

YOU are an instrument in the Lord's hand. YOU are the person providing the blanket—the warmth of the gospel, nurturing and surrounding each young man with the support of loving parents and quorum advisers.

YOU stand on the shore warning young men to stay away from the edge of the Devil's Churn. YOU invite each young man to find the trail to testimony, the trail that will lead him to Christ.

Appendix

Answers to Name the Source Questions

1a *Webelos Handbook,* page 257

1b *For the Strength of Youth,* page 37

2a *Venturer Handbook,* page 79 (paraphrased)

2b *For the Strength of Youth,* page 36

3a *For the Strength of Youth,* page 36

3b *Boy Scout Handbook,* page 394

4a *For the Strength of Youth,* page 36

4b *Boy Scout Handbook,* page 388

5a *Boy Scout Handbook,* page 376

5b *For the Strength of Youth,* page 26

6a *For the Strength of Youth,* page 12

6b *Boy Scout Handbook,* page 370

7a *Boy Scout Handbook,* page 53

7b *For the Strength of Youth,* pages 22–23

Spiritual Impressions